NORTH AMERICAN SALTWATER
FISHING

NORTH AMERICAN SALTWATER FISHING

AL RISTORI

GALLERY BOOKS
An imprint of W.H. Smith Publishers Inc.
112 Madison Avenue
New York, New York 10016

A QUINTET BOOK
produced for
GALLERY BOOKS
An imprint of W. H. Smith Publishers Inc.
112 Madison Avenue
New York, New York 10016

ISBN 0-8317-6434-1

This book was designed and produced by
Quintet Publishing Limited
6 Blundell Street
London N7 9BH

Creative Director: Peter Bridgewater
Art Director: Ian Hunt
Designer: Jonathan Roberts
Project Editor: Judith Simons
Editor: Kate Chambers

Typeset in Great Britain by
Central Southern Typesetters, Eastbourne
Manufactured in Hong Kong by
Regent Publishing Services Limited
Printed in Hong Kong by
South Sea Int'l Press Ltd.

ACKNOWLEDGMENTS

The majority of photographs used in this publication
were supplied by the author, Al Ristori. The author
and publishers would also like to thank the following
for their contribution: Joel Arrington, State of
North Carolina, page 53 r; Buzz Ramsey, Luhr
Jensen Tackle Co., p76 l; and Shimano Corp., pages
54 b, 69 t, 79.

CONTENTS

Introduction

THE LURE OF SALTWATER FISHING

hat is the lure of saltwater fishing? For every angler there may well be a different answer, but there's never been any question in my mind as to why I vastly prefer the call of the sea. Basically, it's the variety and size of the species plus the uncertainty provided by boundless waters.

Any freshwater body of water, no matter how large, is severely restricted. Most have physical boundaries, and even rivers are restricted by their fresh waters that form a barrier to most of the world's fish life. All too often these days there is a sense of artificiality about freshwater fishing; in many cases the freshwater angler seeks hatchery-raised fish not very wise in the ways of the world. There seems to be a certain important element of sport fishing lost when we no longer seek that which nature alone provides. However, that is not to say that great freshwater fishing does not exist.

My own angling adventures started as a youngster growing up in Merrick, a village on Long Island only about 20 miles from the border of New York City. Merrick was still quite rural in those days. A 10-year-old could be trusted to ride his bike to a pond where the glories of fishing awaited in the form of a stunted population of sunfish that rarely exceeded four inches. Those sunnies were tempted to worms which we dug ourselves, and the tackle was even more basic – a bamboo pole with a few feet of string, a float and a tiny hook. The capture of a "huge" 7½-inch sunfish one day sent my buddy and I scurrying back to his house in order to throw it on the bathroom scale, where, alas, my monster did not register at all!

That was probably one of the factors which expanded my horizons to the tidal creek into which Camman's Pond flowed through a pipe. White perch and alewives were lured to the fresh water for spawning purposes in the spring, and those fish appeared absolutely gigantic in comparison to the sunfish. Then again, there were eels in that tidal creek that could weigh well over a pound! From there we went to local docks that provided a variety of young-of-the-year species during the summer that fascinated us. In addition to the targeted "snapper" blues, there were also baby weakfish and even such tropical species as grunts – plus the occasional eel or ugly toadfish.

Eventually we graduated to primitive and very inexpensive revolving spool reels that backlashed on every cast, but Bill and I would spend the family days at Jones Beach by wading into the surf as far as we could go before attempting to cast over the first breaker with a short boat rod. Then we'd have to pick out the backlash before a blowfish would strip our precious bait from the hook.

It wasn't until I was an eighth-grader that I was presented with a home-made bamboo surf rod by a kindly neighbor. Another neighbor would take me along on Saturday morning surf-fishing trips, but it was still all small fish until I landed a 10-pound skate – a trash fish to anyone else, but the greatest treasure of my life to that point. There was surely nothing to compare in the freshwaters of Long Island!

My boat fishing started before that catch, though it was just a

OPPOSITE First light on Shagwong Reef at Montauk, New York – a perfect time to troll for big striped bass when the tide is right.

ABOVE *The author, Al Ristori, with a very large horse-eye jack, a resident of the reefs and inshore channels of Florida, and more commonly the Bahamas.*

TOP *Al Ristori fights a blue shark alongside off Montauk, New York.*

ABOVE *The author's 405-pound mako shark goes up on the scales at Montauk Marine Basin at the end of the day. It was caught from a Mako-22 boat on a small game rod-and-reel combo with 30-pound mono after a 1¾ hour fight.*

rowboat trip with my Uncle Bob (who was a fisherman) and my father who knew nothing about the sport. In those days, few fishermen owned outboard motors. Most casual anglers rented rowboats that were towed to bay fishing grounds. Only a few blowfish and flounders were caught on hand lines that day, but a new world of adventure was opened up to me.

Though I've since caught most of the major (and many of the minor) game fish of the world, my fascination with the oceans and the fish that live in them remains unabated. I still enjoy every facet of the sport, right from bottom fishing for such panfish as flounders up to chunking for giant tuna. No one aspect of saltwater fishing holds a grip on me (though my charter customers force me to devote most of my summer seasons to sharks and tuna), and I particularly enjoy working lures or baits on wrecks or reefs and in remote tropical waters just to see what odd creatures may be encountered. Again, this type of experience is just not available in freshwater.

With no one to guide me, it took many years to attain my present level of fishing experience. The fishing magazines of my youth were filled with "Me and Joe" type stories that inspired but didn't teach. What a difference today! My children have been using rods and reels since they were old enough to handle them. At the tender age of seven, Michael was not only able to go boat fishing on the ocean, but even jigged and subdued a 10½-pound bluefish all by himself. Only two years later, he was mating for me as I guided charter parties to sharks and tuna.

It's a very different world for those breaking into saltwater fishing these days. There may not be as many fish to be caught, but the average angler is far better off than in the "good old days" of greater abundance because the boats, tackle, electronics and readily available information permit us to search out concentrations wherever they exist. No longer are we restricted to areas close to the dock. If the fish don't come to us, we go to them – even if that requires trips of 50 to 100 miles or more. In the future, even what we're doing now will appear quite routine.

Most important of all is that readily available information. When I was a youngster, it was all experimentation. Now you can read this volume and learn all you need to get started. Then you can read newspaper fishing columns and weekly fishing magazines to keep up with the fishing scene, while sharpening your skills through national magazines such as *Salt Water Sportsman, Fishing World* and *Sport Fishing* plus many regional publications and books covering every speciality. If you're a boater, there are now charts that list just about every fishing ground and wreck in your area – and provide Loran C numbers for them, plus courses and distances from your inlet. And, best of all, you can join a fishing club to meet those who have the one indispensible ingredient in successful fishing – local knowledge. (See Chapter 4 for more guidelines on self-tuition.)

If the saltwater opportunities are so much greater now for those just becoming saltwater fishermen, so too are the challenges. It wasn't many years ago that some marine biologists were talking about the virtually unlimited capacity of the oceans. The development of giant stern trawlers, and mother ships to follow them around the oceans, changed that thinking. Those vessels arrived off North American coasts in the 1960s and rapidly depleted the most abundant species from the richest fishing grounds in the world. Cod, haddock, herring, mackerel, red hake, silver hake and other species were devastated by foreign trawler fleets in the North Atlantic, as were many North Pacific bottom fish. At the same time American purse seiners swept the seas from California in search of the tunas that had long before been depleted in local waters. In just a couple of years, the western Atlantic stock of bluefin tuna was reduced from virtually untapped abundance to a population that has recently been only about 10 percent of what it was – even after a decade of controls.

The need for conservation is a critical problem which every saltwater angler must face up to in the future. Marine sportsmen are finally organizing effectively and, in recent years, have managed to reverse the declines of such species as the red drum (redfish) and spotted sea trout in the Gulf Coast states with closed seasons, no netting or no sale laws. A steady decrease in the Atlantic migratory striped bass population was reversed when the States (through the Atlantic States Marine Fisheries Commission) worked under a federal mandate to sharply reduce fishing pressure – including a total moratorium in Maryland's prime spawning waters.

The Fishery Management Councils set up under the Magnuson Act (200-mile-limit law) have been generally slow to act, but are finally putting some effective limits on the catch of such species as king and Spanish mackerel, cod and haddock. The Atlantic Billfish Fishery Management Plan constituted a total breakthrough as the federal government set aside for recreational purposes the blue and white marlin, spearfish and sailfish – even though there was no solid scientific proof that they were depleted. Sale of those species is now prohibited in the U.S. simply because the federal government realizes that they are a more valuable resource swimming free to attract anglers (who spend a fortune pursuing them) rather than being sold for pennies a pound. Hopefully, this represents a turnaround in thinking within the National Marine Fisheries Service from exploitation to conservation, and from crisis management to protection, through management, for species that have not yet been depleted.

Conservation of marine resources for sport fishing is relatively new, but it is the wave of the future. It was only about a century ago that our freshwaters were rescued from the greedy few who would net them to the last fish. A century from now, our descendants will wonder why it took us so long to preserve this precious heritage which can provide both food for the country and recreation for millions if properly managed. It's up to each of us to initiate and support efforts to conserve those resources now so our children will be able to enjoy the great sport of saltwater fishing, rather than scratching for what's left and fighting one crisis situation after another.

ABOVE *The author with a large yellowfin chunked on the west bank of Butterfish Hole off Montauk, New York.*

Chapter One
SALTWATER FISHING TACKLE

Saltwater fishing tackle is so diverse that it's difficult to classify as such except in the case of big game gear. Tackle originally intended strictly for saltwater use is often employed in freshwaters for such large species as sturgeon, alligator gar, chinook salmon and muskies – and even the longest surf rods have been pressed into use by anglers seeking large striped bass and catfish from the banks below some Southwestern dams. On the other hand, standard freshwater tackle is regularly used at sea for everything from wading for sea trout and redfish along the Gulf Coast to casting jigs to school dolphin (the fish, not the mammal) well offshore.

The distinctions between fresh- and saltwater tackle aren't quite as sharp as they used to be, largely because all quality tackle is now built to perform quite well even in the marine environment. In the early days of spinning, it was necessary to take apart even the best of light reels and lubricate them to protect parts that would rust quickly in saltwaters. Since such dedication is no longer required, it's now just a question of fishing conditions. If the size of the fish and the type of water being fished are suited to light tackle, then your standard freshwater rig will do the job nicely.

Any type of tackle will work somewhere in saltwater. The old bamboo pole is still a good tool for catching snapper bluefish, even if the more sophisticated beginners of today all seem to have spinning outfits – or even ultra-light spinners. While saltwater fly-fishing is a very small sport when compared with the freshwater variety, there are quite a few anglers who have discovered the joys of using the long wand on everything from small inshore species right up to the smaller billfish. Indeed, those using specialized saltwater fly rods often do better with large tarpon on Florida Keys flats than fishermen trying to deliver heavier lures with spinning or bait-casting gear.

Though it's even difficult to classify tackle by use, the following section should at least provide a starting point.

Big game

Though formerly an "elite" sport, big game fishing has become more readily available to more people. The development of fast and seaworthy center-console boats has opened up the oceans to those of relatively modest means. These open boats can be rigged into efficient sport-fishermen, and used to catch sharks, blue marlin and giant tuna. If you don't own your own boat, party boats take anglers to sea for a modest fare in many areas.

▮ LEVER DRAG REELS ▮

There are two types of big game reels. Lever drag models feature a lever which can instantly be switched from free spool to a preset strike to a preset full drag, or any point in between. This is a great advantage in fishing (such as sharking) where the reel is left in free spool or with

OPPOSITE *The Penn International 130 lever drag reel.*

ABOVE *Conventional star drag reels are far less expensive than lever drag models and can be utilized (in various sizes) for all saltwater boat fishing.*

just a bit of tension on it so the quarry can pick up the bait and run. When the time comes to strike, the lever is thrown forward to provide exactly what has been set in for striking pressure. Should more drag be required as the fight proceeds, the lever can be advanced to the full drag selected. Adjustments back-and-forth can be made in an instant. Lever drag reels also have larger drag surfaces that dissipate heat efficiently and won't seize up in the course of a fight. From a negative point of view, they are much more costly and tend to be rather heavy. Lever drag reels are usually designated by International Game Fish Association (IGFA) line class. Thus you may select a 50 or 80 for blue marlin fishing, and a 130 for giant tuna.

STAR DRAG REEL

The star drag reel is often simply referred to as a "conventional" reel. This revolving spool type is basically the same as a bait-casting reel, but much larger. Though not nearly as efficient for big game fishing as the lever drag, star drag models cost only a fraction as much and are easy to handle for stand-up fishing. They're particularly good for fishing where the reel is left in a preset drag for an immediate hook-up, or where line is worked out in free spool with the angler ready to engage the clutch immediately a fish picks up the bait. However, even under these circumstances, any attempt to increase or decrease drag pressure involves a guessing game when adjusting the star. The drags are usually adequate for the purpose, but very large fish making long runs against tight drags will create so much heat in the tightly packed washers that the reel will seize up if water isn't applied to bring the heat under control.

The size of star drag reels is usually designated by an old system which really doesn't tell you very much from one manufacturer to another. For instance, one manufacturer's 6/0 reel (suitable for school tuna) may carry far more 50-pound line than a 6/0 reel from a different manufacturer. Big game sizes range from 4/0 to 16/0, though 14/0 is the largest size used for giant tuna in this era of thin diameter lines.

The choice between lever drag and star drag reels for big game fishing is a simple one. If you can afford them, choose the lever drag models. If not, you may be able to mix the two. However, even using only star drag reels you'll be in good shape once you learn to deal with their limitations. In fact, my largest giant tuna was boated on a star drag reel.

Gear ratios on big game reels are generally low in order to provide the required power. Unfortunately, that becomes a problem when large quantities of line have to be retrieved. Until recently, the only company with two-speed reels was Fin-Nor, the Cadillac of the field, whose giant tuna reel with 3:1 and 1:1 ratios was ideal for the task. However, others are now making dual-ratio models that afford a huge advantage with a relatively high ratio for most purposes and a very low one for use when a large fish is straight up-and-down – that is, when it is directly below the boat.

ABOVE *The author waits for giant tuna to strike while trolling off Prince Edward Island, Canada, using lever drag reels.*

OPPOSITE *This 1022-pound giant tuna (the first 1000-pound fish caught on rod-and-reel in the Metropolitan New York area) was caught using a Penn 14/0 star drag Senator reel.*

ABOVE *The author is using standard big game tackle to work a giant tuna from a fighting chair.*

▌RODS ▌

Big game rods used to be pretty much all the same. They were all "trolling" models in the 6½- to 7-foot class with detachable butts. The butts were originally made of wood (which often broke), but are now almost all aluminum or fiberglass. Such rods are still well suited for sitting in a fighting chair to do battle. The long, parabolic-action tips are designed to clear the corners of the boat, and the leverage isn't much of a problem when you're seated.

On the other hand, such rods work against you while fighting a fish standing up – which is the way big game fish should be fought whenever possible in order for the angler to achieve the full measure of satisfaction from the catch. To overcome that leverage problem, fishermen sailing aboard long-range party boats out of San Diego, California, figured they needed shorter, fast-taper rods for wrestling in (from a standing position) yellowfin tuna that may exceed 300 pounds. The result was the development of big game rods that were 5½ feet or less in length with relatively light tips that bend right into an extended foregrip. These usually one-piece models have shorter, very powerful butts which allow the angler to put tremendous pressure on the quarry without ruining his own back. It took a while for stand-up rods to spread from the West Coast, but their advantages are so obvious that few fishermen have resisted the trend.

Big game rods are designated by IGFA line classes. Trolling rods are usually specifically made for a single line class (such as 80 pound), while the stand-up models will handle a wide range of lines (such as 50 to 130 pound). Though graphite has found its way into big game rods, fiberglass (particularly E-glass) is still the favored material for rods subjected to the greatest strains in angling.

▌ GUIDES ▌

Without going into great detail about every aspect of big game rods, it is important to make note of the guides. High quality roller guides are favored for most big game fishing. Provided the angler cleans and lubricates them occasionally in order to keep them turning, there is nothing more efficient than roller guides for preserving your line in the course of a battle with a large game fish. Rollers provide outstanding heat dissipation, but do require that minimum of attention, are relatively expensive and may inhibit the flow of a double line or leader knot through the guides.

At present, the next best thing for big game guides is silicon carbide. This material resembles aluminum oxide, but is more durable and has better heat dissipation qualities. Silicon carbide guides cost only a bit less than rollers, but do provide that large area through which to reel double lines or leaders.

Boat tackle

This is a very broad category which covers the conventional, revolving spool reels and relatively short rods used primarily for fishing from boats and piers in saltwater.

▌ REELS ▌

The standard "conventional" reel is almost always a star drag model, though a few lever drags have been introduced in this class. Penn has completely dominated the boat reel field throughout my adult life, and that American-made product has been so dominant in the lower price classes that they've had virtually no competition in recent years. However, there is now some competition from Shimano, Daiwa, ABU-Garcia and Newell in the higher price classes.

Conventional reels used for boat fishing do not have to be quite as well balanced as others since most aren't intended for casting. Even when casting is necessary, it usually isn't important to get a great deal of distance. Overhand casting is prohibited (for safety reasons) on most party boats, so experienced anglers soon become expert at underhand casting that can put a jig or sinker quite a distance away from competing lines. However, a practiced thumb is required if you're to avoid constant backlashes with this technique.

In addition to lever drags, some of the higher priced models now feature graphite sideplates and one-piece frames for both strength and lightness. Level-wind models are available, and are favored in some bay areas and by a percentage of fishermen trolling with wire line.

The selected boat reel should balance with the rod and have adequate capacity for the fishing. In most cases, fishermen choose boat

TOP *An angler uses a Sabre 5½-foot stand-up rod to fight a school tuna with the aid of a rod belt.*

ABOVE *Party boat anglers use conventional reels to catch such game and food fish as this big pollock, jigged off a Nantucket wreck.*

ABOVE *The late Dave Bowring used his favorite bait-casting tackle to catch this fine weakfish from Peconic Bay, New York.*

reels that are quite a bit larger than they need for most of their normal fishing in order to use the same model on the occasional trolling or deep-sea trip. However, that means holding more weight than necessary throughout most of your fishing – which doesn't make sense.

Boat reel gear ratios are usually low in order to provide power for bottom fishing or to crank-in trolled fish. However, you will want faster retrieve models for casting (particularly if you plan to work popping plugs or retrieve metal lures at high speeds for such species as wahoo and tuna) and jigging.

▌ RODS ▌

Boat rods range from about 5½ to 7 feet, with most being 6 to 6½ feet. Traditionally, they have had detachable wooden butts – but many now are one-piece with the blank running through the butt for strength. Actions vary from very light for bay fishing to more club-like where extra-heavy sinkers are required to hold bottom in deep water. In most cases it's the conditions, more than the size of the quarry, which determine the preferred rod action. Rods are rated by the size ranges of the lures and weights they'll handle, and the angler should pay close attention to that classification when making a selection.

Most boat rods are made of hollow fiberglass, though quite a few now incorporate some graphite. The latter material is most effective when used in the butt section to add stiffness. Solid glass rods are very common in this category as the material is inexpensive. Solid rods are heavy and have poor actions, but are also almost unbreakable – making them ideal for party boat rentals. Since solids are built to sell in low price ranges, they tend to be equipped with the cheapest of components.

▌ GUIDES ▌

Whereas stainless steel guides have been virtually eliminated from freshwater rods, they remain very popular in saltwater – particularly on the West Coast. Tungsten carbide tips are often added to such rods, as the guide takes most of the abuse from monofilament lines. Tungsten carbide is also the standard for all guides when wire line is used, as steel guides will be quickly cut by the metal line. Aluminum oxide guides (the norm in freshwater) have been catching on, and some of the best rods feature silicon carbide guides.

Saltwater bait-casting

The same bait-casting rigs used by just about every bass fisherman in freshwater can be utilized in the briny. However, it's best to set aside the tiny capacity bait-casters with all the gimmicks and go back to the basics. Larger capacity bait-casting reels with wide-ranging star drags are recommended, and it's helpful to have a click on them if you are fishing with bait or trolling. The lightweight spools may not stand up to fish which run off great lengths of mono, as contracting mono can crush such spools. Anglers using bait-casting reels for tarpon in

the Florida Keys usually buy special spools that will stand up under such strains. An alternative is to back the spool with some braided line to absorb the pressure. This isn't usually necessary for the most common saltwater use of bait-casting reels – casting for redfish, sea trout, snook and other small game fish in shallow waters along the Gulf Coast.

A few large bait-casting reels are made specifically for saltwater use. The ABU-Garcia Ambassadeur 7000 and its derivatives are examples of this type, which feature larger capacities in reels still finely tuned for level-wind casting. This size is perfect for a wide range of saltwater fishing – from bottom species to tarpon and amberjack.

Those 5½-foot one-handed freshwater casting rods with the fancy butts aren't very practical for saltwater use, where distance and accuracy is often more important. In addition, the mechanisms on offset reel seats, which lock the reel in, often freeze up in saltwater. Marine anglers usually choose rods with longer, straight butts that can be used with two hands. In addition, the rods tend to be longer – particularly the light-tipped popping rods (usually about 7 feet) popular for wade fishing along the Gulf Coast. On the other hand, I get a great deal of use from muskie rods. These are short (about 5½ feet), stiff rods designed for casting heavy lures to large freshwater fish. They fit easily into a rod case, and I use them with the largest bait-casting reels when traveling to many areas of the world.

Saltwater spinning

Freshwater one-handed spinning rigs will work just fine under many saltwater circumstances, though the marine angler generally prefers longer butts and one-piece models even when fishing with light tackle. Two-piece rods don't become common until lengths go beyond 7 or 8 feet. It's those longer rods and large reels which are usually referred to as saltwater spinning types.

Spinning differs from conventional fishing in that the open-face reel is used under the rod, and reeled with the weak hand so that the fish can be fought with the stronger hand on the rod. Saltwater spinning rods have long butts for two-handed casting, and generally utilize aluminum oxide or stainless steel guides. Boat and jetty models are those in the 7- to 8-foot class which are suitable for the short casts made around jetties (where the fish are apt to be close to the rocks) or from a boat. Once again, there's no point in carrying around more weight than necessary – especially if you're casting all the time. Surf rods range from 8- to 12-feet in one- and two-piece versions – and there are even a few up to 15 feet in three pieces. Anglers casting lures opt for the shortest models practical for the job so as not to wear themselves out. The longer, heavier rods are most suitable for casting large baits and sinkers – and are often left stuck in a sand spike.

Spinning reels should be balanced to the rods, with medium spinners on 7- to 9-footers and large-capacity models on those used for heavy-

ABOVE Closed-face spinning reels are generally not very practical for saltwater use, but these virtually foolproof reels are ideal for getting youngsters started.

RIGHT This dolphin was caught on a fly rod in the Gulf Stream off North Carolina.

duty bait fishing in the surf or boat trolling and bottom fishing. Spinning reels are easy to cast, but have no advantage when it comes to trolling or bottom fishing. Indeed, their inherent lack of power mitigates against their use in those areas. However, some southeast Florida skippers like to use them when trolling live baits for sailfish in order to get a quick and completely free drop-back when a fish hits.

Saltwater fly-fishing

The basics of fly-fishing don't change as you go from freshwater to saltwater, but there is a big difference in the tackle. The light wands used to cast tiny dry flys in creeks have little application in the marine environment, and the simple single-action fly reels that are quite adequate for trout aren't designed to stand up to either saltwater or the larger, stronger fish which may be encountered. Specialized saltwater fly reels (such as the Fin-Nor and Seamaster) are primarily handmade and quite expensive, though the largest Pflueger Medalists and Scientific Anglers System Two models will also do the job for everything short of big game.

Drags are hardly a concern in most freshwater fly-fishing, but they're very important in the briny. An anti-reverse mechanism is also advisable when larger species are sought. The rods are generally longer and heavier, which enables the angler to cast large, wind-resistant flys a considerable distance. Nine-footers capable of handling forward-taper lines from number 8 to 13 are fairly standard in saltwater areas (even lead-core line is used in specialized cases,) and they are normally equipped with short butt extensions that can be plugged in quickly in the act of fighting a fish. While graphite hasn't come to dominate in other saltwater rod types, it is generally the preferred fly-rod material with its combination of lightness and backbone. The weight of saltwater fly outfits is a prime consideration, though few marine fly-fishermen engage in blind casting.

ABOVE *Saltwater spinning reels are a popular choice for sailfish when a piece of flexible wire is run from the rod to hold the line from an open bail. When a sailfish hits, the line is pulled free and the fish feels no pressure until the angler flips over the bail and strikes.*

LEFT *Most surfcasters use spinning tackle for striped bass and all other gamesters frequenting the suds.*

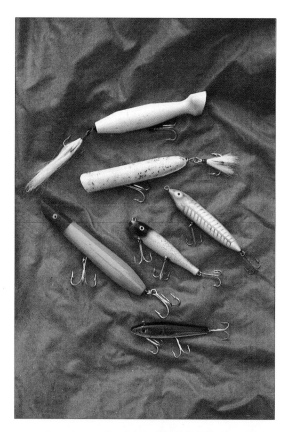

TOP *Surface plugs of many types provide great sport with such species as bluefish, striped bass, amberjack and snook.*

ABOVE *High-speed trolling lures come in many styles.*

Lines

By far the most common line for saltwater use is monofilament, along with the very similar looking multi-polymers. The minimum visibility provided by these lines has been enhanced by technological improvements that have provided extremely thin diameters per pound-test. Thus, smaller reels can be filled with the same yardage of a particular test that was formerly only used on a heavier model – this saves the angler both wear and tear on his arm and a few dollars. This has become most obvious in the big game area, where a drop of one size in a reel makes a big difference in price and may permit stand-up fishing with lines that were formerly considered strictly suitable for use by fishermen in fighting chairs. For instance, 50-pound big game reels, which are light enough for stand-up fishing, are now regularly used with 80-pound and even 100-pound thin monos for tunas that may run up to 300 pounds or more.

It should be emphasized that every monofilament or multi-polymer line is a bundle of compromises. When too much of one desirable property is developed, you'll generally lose some of another. Thus, the angler should consider the type of fishing he is doing before selecting a line which is extra thin, or one which has a minimum of stretch, or another with excellent abrasion resistance. Colors are a matter of personal preference, though certain colors do seem to blend in better in various areas. Clear is a safe selection, while pink, blue and green are often preferred.

Stretch is a problem inherent in monofilament and multi-polymers, but it also has some advantages. Though stretch is a disadvantage when jigging a lure or setting a hook, it also acts as a shock absorber, making it difficult to break the line at a distance even when mistakes are made. On the other hand, braided Dacron brings stretch down to about 10 percent. This makes broken lines so common in the lighter classes that Dacron isn't used much anymore except for big game fishing. When a giant tuna has to be pumped up, that lack of stretch is a big advantage. Dacron is also favored for very deep-water bottom fishing. Braided nylon lines have just about disappeared from the saltwater scene, as they were both highly visible and extremely stretchy. Those casting with conventional reels were the last market for the limp and water-absorbent braided nylons, but they too have opted for monofilament in recent years.

Even the addition of lots of trolling sinkers to the above lines will not take them very deep when trolling. Of course, downriggers will serve to bring mono to the depths at which fish may be feeding – but you can accomplish the same thing on a direct basis with wire line or lead core. Wire lines cut through the water and bring your lure down about one foot for every 10 feet of wire streamed. Thus, with 200 feet of wire astern your lure should be working at about 20 feet. Monel is the most supple and least likely to kink of the wire lines, but slightly less expensive stainless steel will also do the job. Braided wire is easier to handle, but doesn't sink as well and can burr. Lead core consists of a flexible lead strip encased in a sheath of Dacron or braided nylon. It's easy to handle, but quite bulky – and doesn't get down well in currents. Lead core is most suitable for relatively shallow bay situations.

Saltwater fly lines are heavier than those intended for freshwater use, and invariably feature a forward taper for maximum casting capabilities. Some companies even put out special saltwater tapers with slight modifications. Sinking lines are more commonly used than floaters, and a length of lead core may be added in special situations to attain necessary depths in currents.

Lures

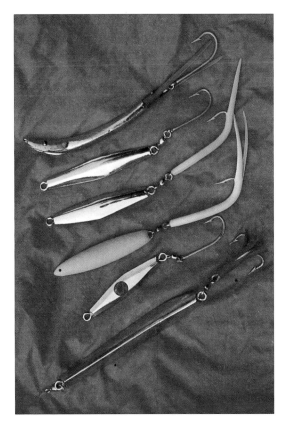

There's such a diversity of saltwater lures, that it's impossible to separate many of them from freshwater models. Indeed, just about any freshwater lure will work somewhere and for something in the briny. I well remember casting a regular freshwater in-line spinning lure among the shallow grass patches in the Gulf of Mexico many years ago and catching a great variety of small fish. Just a few nights later in the Florida Keys, I jumped tarpon from a bridge on a freshwater plug. Those lures and many others intended for bass, pike, muskies and many other sweetwater game fish will work in some saltwater situations, but most have hooks that are too light and will not stand up in the marine environment.

As a general rule, saltwater lures are larger and heavier than freshwater models. Since the pace of life is much quicker in the ocean, retrieves are normally faster – and most lures are designed for such use. Especially notable as strictly oceanic lures are the high-speed offshore models; these lures are trolled at speeds of about 6 to 10 knots on average, and many will work at much greater speeds.

JIGS

Jigs of many types have been devised to work the depths for species ranging from tiny up to hundreds of pounds – and these are probably the single type of lure I'd want in my survival kit. The most common type of jig has a lead head and a hook dressed with bucktail, nylon or other materials. Plastic worms are added to the hooks for species such as weakfish, while southern anglers normally tip them with shrimp or shedder crab. Another popular type is the diamond jig, a fast-sinking chromed-lead lure that may be rigged with just a single or treble hook – or with a tube tail. Diamond jigs are very popular in the Northeast for bluefish, striped bass and cod, and in the Pacific Northwest for halibut and many other bottom species. Most anglers from New Jersey to New England favor diamond jigs with single hooks on swivels, as this type doesn't snag in bottom easily and makes it harder for the quarry to shake the hook. The old-fashioned treble-hooked diamond jig is still preferred by deepwater cod fishermen and those in the Northwest.

Metal casting lures have flatter sides and can be used at all depths. Due to their shape, they don't sink as quickly as diamond jigs – though

TOP *Diamond jigs come in many variations, but all are designed to sink fast and produce a wide range of saltwater fish.*

ABOVE *Bucktail and plastic-bodied lead-head jigs of many sizes are constant producers.*

that can be an advantage in shallow waters. Most lures of this type are chrome-plated, but the most famous of all is the stamped, stainless steel Hopkins.

PLUGS

Saltwater plugs come in many sizes. Large models are favored for big stripers and bluefish, but 100-pound tarpon may be more inclined to take the same small MirrOlure that would also be presented to much smaller species such as snook, sea trout and redfish. Surface lures are the most fun, since the strike can be seen as well as felt. Swimming plugs are worked slowly and provide lots of action, while popping plugs are retrieved at high speed and will often stir up well-fed fish that would pass up more conventional lures.

TUBES

Tubes are unique to saltwater and can be used as lures themselves or as dressing on other lures. Surgical and synthetic tubing caught on as a trolling lure for striped bass, and in many forms these lures now account for huge numbers of bluefish, stripers and weakfish in the Northeast, plus barracuda and cobia in the South. Short tubes are used to arm the most unusual looking lure of all, the umbrella rig. This is a usually four-armed wire rig with a weight in the middle. Tube lures are run directly from the swivel or from leaders from the end of each arm, and smaller teaser tubes are positioned half-way along each arm. Another tube or other lure may also be run down the middle of the rig. Trolled deep on wire line, the umbrella rig imitates a school of sand eels and is rarely outfished by anything else when that bait is present, while also providing multiple catches.

A big game variation of the umbrella rig involves a single bar from which daisy chains of soft plastic squid or mackerel are run. Only the last lure has a hook in it, and the rig is designed to tear off when a giant tuna is hooked. Versions of the same rig with shorter squid are used to troll for smaller tunas. Though very expensive, these rigs enable captains to cut down on fuel costs as they are trolled much slower than high-speed models.

FLIES

Saltwater flies are generally long and bushy compared to freshwater models, though bonefish flies (which usually imitate shrimp) are not very large. Rather than imitating specific insects and hatches as in trout fishing, the saltwater fly-fisherman simply must present something that looks edible – usually an imitation of a bait fish. Thus, the standard saltwater fly is a streamer, which can be anything from a one-inch length for bonito and other small game fish to a foot-long creation for sailfish and marlin. In flats fishing, shrimp and crabs are the usual quarry for bonefish and permit. Therefore, imitations of those crustaceans are most effective. In addition to the usual materials, saltwater fly-fishermen utilize a great deal of mylar and bright artificial hair. Larger, stronger hooks are utilized, and sink rates are often improved by using a heavier hook or adding lead to the hook shank.

ABOVE *Umbrella rigs also produce multiple catches at times, such as this triple-header of two bluefish and one striped bass taken off Sandy Hook, New Jersey.*

Accessories

▮ HARNESSES ▮

Big game anglers require a seat or kidney harness in order to be able to slide back-and-forth in a fighting chair. However, stand-up big game fishing is becoming ever more popular – and that calls for different equipment. Modern rod belts and kidney harnesses have made it possible to exert great pressure on a large fish with the short rods intended for this purpose – and without breaking your back in the process. The harness rests along the lower back and hips, and may be connected to the rod belt with drop straps so the rod pushes against the thighs rather than in the groin area, as they were formerly worn. Stand-up anglers may also use wrist bands and knee pads for added comfort while fighting tuna weighing well over 100 pounds.

▮ GAFFS ▮

Gaffs are a very important item for big game fishing. Straight-handled gaffs with heavy hooks are fine for tuna, which don't spin or jump when hit. However, flying gaffs are preferred for sharks (which spin) and billfish, which may jump. The hook of a flying gaff is separate from the handle, and is inserted into the handle for striking the fish – after which it pulls free and holds the quarry via a line attached to the boat. Some giant-tuna fishermen also carry a cockpit harpoon in order to reach out further for the very valuable bluefin. However, it's important to remember that the use of a harpoon is not allowed under IGFA sport fishing rules – a fish hit with one is disqualified both for record consideration and in any contest run under IGFA rules.

Gaffs are also important for smaller game, but the hooks are proportionally smaller and the handles only 3 to 5 feet, rather than 8 feet, in length. The best bet is to have at least two aboard – one with a heavy hook that won't straighten out on large, powerful fish, and another with a light hook that penetrates easily into smaller fish.

▮ CLOTHING ▮

Foul weather gear is a must for almost every fisherman. Heavy-duty slickers will stand up well in cold weather areas, but southern anglers have to settle for light nylon or vinyl outfits (that tear easily) since heavier suits are just too hot when temperatures are high. Best of all for cold weather fishing is a working survival suit. Though quite expensive, these suits provide warmth and will keep you afloat should an accident occur. Furthermore, it's not necessary to wear foul weather gear over survival suits.

Surfcasters can get by with a bathing suit in the summer, but the best fishing in many areas occurs when cold weather sets in. Waders are more practical than hip boots, and neoprene gloves are a handy item when temperatures drop to freezing point. Wader belts (usually web-type) serve to retain air in the waders and prevent the entrance of water, so you'll float rather than sink. They also provide a means of holding a lure bag for the caster who must maintain mobility. On the

ABOVE *A single long tube trolled on wire line off the New Jersey shore produced this striped bass.*

BELOW A short gaff is sufficient for school bluefin tuna such as this one gaffed off Montauk, New York.

other hand, bait fishermen need sand spikes to hold their reels out of the sand – and may want to carry along a light folding seat.

▓ MISCELLANEOUS ▓

Tackle boxes come in so many sizes and shapes that it's impossible to recommend a single box for universal use in saltwater. Marine anglers should avoid any metal tackle box or cooler. Stick with high-quality synthetic boxes and remember to check that the compartments are large enough to hold your lures.

Other basic accessories for the boat fisherman include fishing pliers, fillet and bait knives, a dehooker, hook honers and scales. Many fishermen don't carry scales, and are always guessing the weights of fish caught – and especially those released. With a fine brass Chatillon Instrument Scale, you'll not only get accurate weights but will also be able to set drags accurately.

Bait fishermen can gather their own sea worms, clams, fiddler crabs and other small creatures on mud and sand flats with Mikie's Bait Catcher, a suction tube device.

Boats and electronics

Just about anything that floats is suitable for saltwater use under some circumstances. I started out as a teenager with a 16-foot wooden lapstake on Long Island, and then used a pirouge (cut from a log) to fish in the Caribbean. After years of working on wooden boats, I was delighted to get into a Starcraft aluminum 16-footer for striper fishing. That lightweight, shallow draft, easily trailered boat was ideal for the bay – but rivets popped out when I dropped off waves while trolling bluefish on the ocean.

It was the development of the relatively inexpensive, center-console fiberglass boat that made it possible for the average angler to fish safely well out to sea and beat most of the larger craft to and from the grounds. I started with a Mako 19, and then went on to Mako 21-, 22- and 25-footers with the same 8-foot beam before advancing to the 9½-foot beam Aquasport 28-1. With these boats I've caught everything from small game up to sharks and giant tuna and they've now become a standard for small boat fishermen on open waters. Indeed, some are outfitted with fighting chairs, outriggers, downriggers, T-tops or tuna towers, drop-down curtains and other items that turn these "open" boats into mini sport-fishermen. Outboards, which have become ever more powerful and dependable, power most such craft, though some boats utilize outdrives or inboard power.

Another type of boat that's become very popular in recent years is the 29- to 31-foot cabin model with a large cockpit plus the speed, fuel capacity and seaworthiness to reach distant fishing areas on day trips or overnighters. The comfort of much larger craft is preferable but these smaller sport-fishermen are perfectly adequate for most offshore fishing situations – and don't cost a fortune to buy, run and maintain.

When I started boat fishing, the most sophisticated equipment carried by most small boaters was a compass. In order to locate a wreck or fishing ground, it was necessary to run a time and course before lining up landmarks. Even when conditions were perfect, a sinker might have to be sacrificed on a drift across the wreck in order to be sure of its exact location before anchoring. Carl Lowrance developed the first inexpensive flasher fishfinder (the portable "little green box"), but it was some years before this miracle spread to the briny with units that could take salt spray. Graph recorders, used by the wealthy since the 1950s, then came down in price and were waterproofed for small boats. To top it off, Loran C become affordable.

LEFT Even giant tuna can be boated from properly equipped small boats, such as the author's original Mako-25 – the fighting chair is situated in the bow.

Now the novice can buy a fishing chart listing the Loran C numbers of almost every likely fishing area, set the numbers into his unit and obtain a course and distance. Those numbers will put him within 50 feet of the spot, and the recorder will then zero it in. You'll still need the skills to anchor or drift properly, and to tempt the fish. However, modern electronics makes it possible for the novice to advance rapidly rather than spending years developing basic fish-locating skills.

A compass, graph, video or LCD (liquid crystal display) fishfinder and Loran C are a must for any serious boater. In addition, you'll need a VHF radio for both safety and fishing information. Another important item is a water temperature gauge. Even slight changes in surface temperatures can mean good fishing or poor – there are often significant temperature variations within a small area. You can utilize a fine Dytek gauge that will give you a readout of time, temperature and loran numbers at the touch of a button when a hit occurs while trolling. Alternatively, some advanced fishfinders give water temperature information. The recent development of small boat radars makes it possible to run safely in the fog without the entire console being taken up with a large unit.

Chapter Two
SALTWATER FISHING SKILLS

Effective use of tackle

The secret to success in big game fishing can be summed up in one word – technique. Very strong anglers are often able to overpower large game fish, but more often they're quickly reduced to a veritable bowl of jelly if they don't succeed in subduing their quarry quite quickly. This doesn't simply apply to people of average strength and years, but even those who are relatively young and work out regularly.

OPPOSITE *This sundown surfcasting scene is at Cape Hatteras, North Carolina.*

ABOVE *Modern stand-up big game tackle enables men and women anglers of limited strength to successfully fight school tuna.*

TECHNIQUE VERSUS STRENGTH

Some years ago I put Jerry Kramer, the famed ex-Green Bay Packer lineman, on a 150-pound class shark off Walker's Cay in the Bahamas during a Mako Marine Outdoor Writer's Tournament. Kramer, who's not only a big man but also a fine freshwater angler, tried to overpower the shark on 50-pound trolling tackle from a standing position in the center-console Mako we were using. However, the shark didn't care for the sight of our boat and took off with a new charge of energy. Kramer had expended his power right away, and ended up having to hang on for a long time before I was finally able to get the wire leader and release the shark. That incident was not unique. I see it repeated time-and-again every year. In fact, most anglers who exhaust themselves quickly give up on the fish and pass the rod to a companion. On one occasion I had all three members of a fishing party on one yellowfin tuna of just a bit over 100 pounds before the first one came back to finish the fight – which lasted only 20 minutes.

On the other hand, by employing the short-stroking technique (developed by West Coast, long-range party boat fishermen), a fellow fishermen of average size successfully wrestled each of six yellowfins – two of which were in the 100-pound class – to the anchored boat within five minutes. Outfitted with a 5½-foot stand-up rod and modern kidney harness with a rod belt, he maintained constant pressure on the tuna as each short pump of the rod resulted in a few more inches of line on the reel. The idea is to avoid the long strokes that make it appear the angler is gaining a lot of line, but actually allow the fish to "get its head" on each downstroke. The short pumps keep the tuna's head up and prevent it from diving to regain its strength.

THE STAND-UP FIGHT

As described in the previous chapter, *Saltwater Fishing Tackle*, stand-up big game tackle and accessories have revolutionized the saltwater fishing world. After years of back-breaking effort while standing up with trolling rods, shoulder harnesses and belly rod belts, the toughest game fish can now be fought in relative comfort and with great efficiency. The 4¾- to 6-foot fast taper, short-butted stand-up rods allow the angler to apply maximum pressure and lift the fish inch-by-inch as it circles below the boat.

Just about any tackle will do when a big game fish makes its initial run.

BELOW *The fine results of stand-up battles with school bluefin tuna off Montauk, New York.*

With the fish away from the boat, you can snap into the harness and lean back on it while gaining line in big chunks when the fish turns or the boat runs on it. However, even then (during the easiest portion of the fight) it's possible to wear yourself out. I've seen many "pumped-up" fishermen wind the reel handle continuously as line is flying off the spool or the weight of the fish prohibits the retrieval of line. The effort involved in doing this will wear out anyone before the real fight begins, and will accomplish nothing.

The short-stroking technique comes into play when the quarry is straight up-and-down. At that point (especially with tuna) the angler must move the unwilling fish to the surface by the efficient application of pressure. Tuna circle continuously under the boat, and each circle provides the opportunity to raise the fish a few inches closer. Don't get caught with your rod tip way up in the air. Instead, concentrate on making short lifts – and be sure to start reeling before dropping the rod tip. All too often I see fishermen go through all the effort of lifting the rod tip, only to then drop it before they ever start reeling. The net result is a great deal of effort expended for no purpose – and such a fisherman will rarely make it through the fight unless he gets coordinated. It's hard to contain your enthusiasm when the biggest and strongest fish you've ever tangled with is pouring line off your reel, but by applying your strength selectively you'll be able both to enjoy the battle and complete it – rather than having to pass the rod over.

IN THE CHAIR

The same basics apply to a sit-down fight. Especially with heavy tackle, it's vital that you don't wear yourself out early. The fish must be fought with the back and legs – not the arms. By pushing back-and-forth in the chair, pressure can be applied and the fish moved so you can take a turn or more on the reel without even using your left arm to hold the rod. A bent butt, big game rod is an asset in most fighting chair situations as it allows for more efficient pumping.

A technique I've found to be very valuable in dealing with giant tuna when double lines are used is to utilize a gloved hand on the double line once it's on the spool. This extra pressure should roll the tuna over and prevent it from getting its head to make another run. The double gives you twice the breaking strength you've been fighting the fish with, and any tuna which isn't "green" (still fresh, with only the dark back showing) should be taken right then and there before it regains its strength and takes off again.

The boat does most of the work in the course of fighting a big game fish from a chair, but the angler is called on to do more from a small boat. With the fighting chair mounted in the bow, the ideal situation is for the fish to tow the boat and tire itself out. However, giant tuna eventually find there's less pressure when they stay directly below the boat. That's when the angler must really go to work. Most small-boat chairs have no foot rests, and the angler uses the inside of the gunwale to obtain a purchase for pumping the fish up. With the chair in the bow, the skipper keeps track of the fight while looking forward, and can easily hold the fish away from the props and trim tabs at the stern.

PARTY BOAT FISHING

Party boat anglers must make some adjustments in order to fight big game fish. Movement is a must, particularly when the party boat is anchored – which is usually the case. The idea, just as with smaller game, is to move with the fish so as to keep it directly in front of you. By doing that, you'll be able to avoid a cut-off should the quarry make a sudden move in any direction and you'll also usually prevent tangling with other anglers' lines. When a fish suddenly makes a run from bow to stern or vice-versa, the angler or crew member should take the rod by the end of the butt, point it straight down, and run from one point to the other. It's important for anglers to release the reel from harness straps at boatside in order to make the last minute moves with the rod tip necessary to prevent loss under the boat. Fish are moved to one corner of the stern or the other in order to avoid tangling with the props and rudder in the middle. The most critical moves in party boat big game fishing involve getting the rod under the anchor line when the fish circles the bow. This invariably involves at least two people, one to hold the rod under the taut line and the other to get a firm grip on it from the opposite side. The basic rules apply to party boat fishing in general. Always follow your fish in order to avoid most of the tangles which are a prime headache in this sport. Light tackle is great sport and often more effective in hooking fish, but the party boat fisherman must use some reason in deciding what can be used under the circumstances. What may be appropriate with a small weekday party may not be reasonable on a crowded weekend.

While small boat anglers can usually avoid being stripped by an

ABOVE *Frank Mather, the marine scientist who instigated bluefin tuna tagging and led the way to the conservation of this over-exploited species, demonstrates the use of the legs and body to fight a giant tuna – a technique that reduces the strain on the angler. Notice that he isn't even using his left hand on the rod while reeling with his right.*

LEFT *The angler is pulled upright as a giant tuna fights against a heavy drag.*

unexpectedly big fish simply by buoying their anchor line and drifting or running after the fish, the shore and pier fisherman is much more restricted. Therefore, he must be sure that his reel capacity is sufficient for the fish he may encounter. Surfcasters regularly try to cast to the horizon, but fish are often feeding right in the wash – and that area should not be overlooked. Even more so, those working jetties should spend much of their time casting alongside the rocks which are a natural attraction for many game and bottom fish.

Light-tackle fishermen should learn from their big-game brethren and utilize a pumping technique when working in large fish – and those using spinning tackle must take special care not to turn the reel handle when line is going out or none is being retrieved. Whereas the latter merely saps strength when using revolving spool reels, on spinning reels every turn of the handle under such circumstances puts a twist in the monofilament. After a while, the line becomes so twisted as to be virtually unusable until straightened out. This can be accomplished by cutting off all terminal tackle and running the line out astern of a moving boat.

LEFT *The wrong combination of wind, swell and tide can make even very safe inlets, such as at Manasquan, New Jersey, risky for boaters.*

RIGHT *The anchor ball can be used to float the anchor allowing relatively effortless retrieval. The anchor ball is tied to the end of the anchor line so it can be cast off when a large tuna is hooked.*

SETTING THE DRAG

One important point that applies to all fishing involves the drag. Drags are best set with a good spring scale, such as the Chatillon Instrument Scale. The true test of drag is off the rod tip, not directly from the reel, and most fishermen will probably find that their drags are set too light when they actually test them. As a general rule, set your strike position at about 20 percent of line breaking strength, and push that up to 33 percent for full drag. Even more drag can be applied in special situations, such as tuna fishing.

Set your drag before you start fishing, and then stick with it. For some reason, many saltwater fishermen panic when they watch line being pulled off their reel. Instead of holding the rod high and making the fish use maximum energy in the course of that run, they instinctively screw down the drag to stop the run. Not surprisingly, that sudden shock in stopping a fast-running fish frequently results in a

broken line. You would almost believe that some people figure the reel is filled with line just so there'll be some left when they screw down the drag and break off!

Increasing drag is something you generally don't want to do, because drag automatically increases as the amount of line on the spool decreases. Though there are times you'll want to add pressure, it is better to do it with your hands rather than the reel. Finger pressure can be applied lightly to the spool or to the line against the foam or cork foregrip of the rod. That added pressure is often necessary in order to pump up a big fish. The sheer weight of the fish may pull line from the reel, and all your pumping could be for naught unless you prevent that with some finger pressure.

Analyzing fishing conditions

The saltwater angler must deal with even more variables than his freshwater counterpart. Though all of us are frustrated by situations where conditions are perfect but the fish still don't cooperate, the successful fisherman is usually one who takes all the natural factors into account and puts himself "in the right place, at the right time."

WEATHER, TIDES AND CURRENTS

Weather is one of the prime variables. It determines both where and whether we'll be fishing, and has a similar powerful influence on the fish we seek. For instance, a storm featuring large ground swells may ruin inshore bottom fishing in ocean areas for days thereafter due to turbidity on the bottom – but surface feeders could go on a rampage under the same conditions. It will take a while before you become familiar with weather effects in your area, but that knowledge will save some wasted trips.

Tides and currents are vital factors in saltwater fishing. Most species feed when there is a current running but shut off in slack water. However, there are many exceptions to that rule, particularly in bottom fishing when currents are strong. On any given day, certain species may hit on one tide but not the other. Usually this relates to bait movements, but there are occasions when bait is abundant on both tides while game fish feed on only one. Currents are equally important far offshore, where a shift can bring in warmer or cooler water and either help or hinder angling. Offshoots of the Gulf Stream, called eddies, often provide outstanding fishing in the canyons of the Northeast. The rise and fall of the tides changes the nature of inshore fishing grounds. Prime high tide spots may be too shallow, or even out of water, on low tide. This is particularly critical in Florida Keys flats fishing. Guides there study tide charts to determine which flats will have enough water on them to attract bonefish and permit. The greater rise and fall of the tide around the full and new moons has a profound effect on fishing. Currents will be stronger at these periods, and fish may react in various ways. For instance, big game fishermen usually dislike the full moon period – but that is the prime time for blue marlin fishing off St. Thomas in the Virgin Islands. For striped bass fishermen, the full moon signals the best period for catching trophy bass at night.

▌ USING YOUR SENSES ▐

The key to successful saltwater fishing involves bringing all your senses into play. The sense of smell can play an important role. For example, in the course of feeding, slicks are created by such species as bluefish and the tunas – and those slicks give off a "watermelon" odor. After you get used to scenting that odor, you'll even be able to tell how fresh it is. The stronger the odor, the more likely that the predators are still close to the slick. Look for them upwind or upcurrent of the slick itself.

Sight is obviously an important sense, as in almost every type of saltwater fishing there are visual clues that can lead you to better sport simply by observing and understanding them. I once owned a trailered 16-foot Starcraft aluminum boat which not only lacked any electronics but even a compass. However, I used to search out bluefish primarily by smelling the previously noted slicks or observing them visually. The sense of smell worked well when I was downwind of them, but half the slicks would have gone unnoticed if I hadn't sighted them upwind. A single jumping fish or swirl has often put me into an entire school. Spotting a weed line or a floating piece of wood can make the difference between a skunking and a huge catch of dolphin.

Tidal movements over high spots on the bottom are a powerful fish attraction, and there is usually some indication on the surface as to the existence of some kind of structure below. In shallower areas, a rip line forms on the surface when the tide is running – particularly when the wind is blowing against the current. Predators gather at the base of the rip to grab bait fish being swept over the structure, and anglers can troll lures at that edge (usually with wire line to bring the lure to the feeding depth) or fish it with jigs by drifting across or by stemming the tide and dropping jigs back into the pay-off zone.

Flats fishing in the Florida Keys is almost strictly a sighting experience. Guides pole along the flats and spot cruising bonefish, permit, tarpon, barracuda and blacktip sharks before the angler makes a cast. Polarized glasses should be standard for fishermen as they cut the glare and allow you to see below the surface. Bonefish and permit often stick their tails out of the water while rooting out crabs and shrimp in shallow waters. Surprisingly, "tailers" can be spotted quite well at dawn and dusk.

Californians spot their striped marlin by scanning the water for tails sticking out of the water. Unlike the other marlins, most striped marlin are sighted before being baited. The same applies to trolling for swordfish. Very few of those fish have been taken by blind trolling. However, surfacing swordfish will sometimes take a bait trolled in front of them and then dropped there.

The surfcaster must be particularly aware of what lies before him. A

BELOW Flats guides, such as Captain Rick Ruoff of Islamorada, Florida, pole the flats at specific stages of the tide to seek out bonefish, permit, tarpon, barracuda and other species.

OPPOSITE The author fishes for dolphin next to a sargassum weed patch floating in the Gulf Stream off North Carolina. Dolphin and many other warm-water species are attracted to any floating object at sea, and they should always be checked out.

blind cast may leave his bait sitting on a bar in water too shallow to attract game. fish. Check the beach out at low tide so you can determine where the various cuts in the bars are, and then fish those cuts (which are natural passageways for game fish) on the higher tides. Soon you'll be able to analyze wave movement to determine where the deeper spots are.

Always keep your ears open while on the water. An unseen splash may lead you to a concentration of fish. I've fished quiet bays and creeks on many dark nights when my primary clue as to where to cast a lure for striped bass or weakfish was the sound of a splash or swirl.

▮ BIRD CLUES ▮

One of the most obvious clues to sight is bird action. It takes some experience to tell the difference between birds "looking" and birds "working," but you'll soon get the hang of it. Birds diving on the water usually signal the presence of game fish below, though there are occa-

ABOVE *Darrell Lowrance, president of Lowrance Electronics, holds one of the big striped bass taken while night fishing with the aid of the weatherproof Lowrance graph recorder on the console behind him.*

RIGHT *Sundown is a prime time for spotting tailing bonefish, such as here on the flats at Islamorada, Florida.*

sions (particularly on slack water) when schools of bait fish will rise to the surface and provide easy pickings despite a lack of feeding predators. Even birds sitting on the water can be a clue to future activity: they may be hanging around bait fish, and there could be action when some condition changes. Ordinarily, it's flocks of birds you'll be looking for. However, a single bird may spot a fish close by before the others zero in. The frigate, or man-o'-war bird is a good solo indicator of big fish below in offshore waters. That bird can't dive, and must rely on bait fish being chased into the air or left crippled. Lacking any other better clues, it's a good idea to troll the area under the frigate.

▌ A FEEL FOR ROD AND LINE ▌

All of the foregoing becomes part of acquiring a feel for fishing. The rod in your hand should become a part of your body, and what you feel through it will determine how a lure must be worked – or whether there's still bait on your bottom rig. Successful bottom fishing and

ABOVE *Working birds are a sure sign that game fish are below.*

RIGHT *This small tarpon was landed on the rocks next to a Florida Keys bridge while night fishing. It was released to fight another day.*

jigging requires that you have a good feel of bottom. Fishermen who can't feel the slacking as a jig or sinker hits bottom, and can't get the hang of maintaining a tight line contact with bottom as they drop back in response to the current, won't do well in the sport. I always keep my fingers on the line to feel anything which would give me an indication of what might be going on below.

Though rods are normally placed in holders for trolling, I usually hold my rod while trolling inshore waters – particularly with wire line. This enables me to get a feel for how the lure should be working, and I can compensate in boat speed for variations in the currents throughout the tide. Furthermore, I'll know if I hit bottom and must "shorten up," or if I've picked up a bit of weed that will make the lure ineffective. Best of all, I'll be able to feel the slightest bump on the lure – and the arm-wrenching smash of a jumbo striped bass, which is the highlight of the fight as far as I'm concerned.

The sense of feel is particularly vital if casting lures. You must acquire the touch in retrieving lures at the correct rate both for the type of lure under the circumstances and for the species you're seeking. On a dark night you may have nothing to work with but your sense of feel in determining whether your lure is working correctly. Some fish, such as the tunas and mackerels, require a fast retrieve while others prefer a slow-moving lure. By varying your retrieve, it may be possible to pick out more desirable species with the same lure in a given area. For instance, an angler using a diamond jig during the fall migratory period in the Mid-Atlantic area can often catch unlimited numbers of big bluefish with a fast retrieve. However, by just taking a couple of slow turns off bottom and pausing before dropping the jig back to bottom, it may be possible to reduce the number of bluefish hits while picking up some more desirable striped bass and weakfish.

RECORD-KEEPING

Something that's worked well for me and should be copied by every angler is record keeping. Being able to refer back to records of every fishing trip over the years will provide information that can make you a better angler. Perhaps more important than that is the opportunity to re-live memories of trips – with all the details correctly stated. Record-keeping will also enable you to compete against yourself. In this age of big money fishing tournaments, there's a lot of controversy about their effect on the sport. However, regardless of your feelings about competitive fishing, there can be nothing but pleasure involved in trying to outdo yourself in catching the biggest and the greatest number (hopefully released) over the years. There's no need for a fancy journal (a simple notebook will do), and you'll soon find that it's easy to keep track of the catch in your head during a day of fishing. Carry an accurate scale (such as the Chatillon Instrument Scale) with you at all times, so even released fish can be weighed.

By combining the use of all your senses along with a knowledge of the conditions and the species sought, you can be among the 10 percent of saltwater fishermen who catch 90 percent of the fish!

TOP *Electronics permit experienced boaters to fish offshore in even thick fog – providing catches such as this giant tuna caught off Block Island, Rhode Island.*

ABOVE *Surfcasters working in confused surf at Cape Point, Hatteras, North Carolina.*

Chapter Three

MAJOR SALTWATER SPECIES

cquiring knowledge about the species you seek is not only rewarding in itself, but can make you a better fisherman. Clues as to where the fish will be, plus how and what they'll be feeding on, are all available in descriptions of the species' life style. By understanding the quarry and its habits, you'll be equipped to seek it in a more efficient manner.

The descriptions provided here are necessarily brief, but will provide you with some basic information about the major groups of game and food fish plus some of the more unusual species to be encountered off the continental United States and Canadian coasts. Brief mentions are made of a few species which may be caught in Hawaii and those which are very rare to the north but are abundant in Caribbean or Central American waters. The range specification is limited in most cases to the species' occurrence in North American waters only. Scientific names are provided in order to prevent confusion with other similar species. Some excellent reference books are available for those seeking more detailed information on various species.

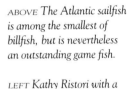

ABOVE *The Atlantic sailfish is among the smallest of billfish, but is nevertheless an outstanding game fish.*

LEFT *Kathy Ristori with a very large white marlin (99½ pounds) caught while sharking off Montauk, New York.*

OPPOSITE *When excited, striped marlin take on a distinctive neon-blue coloration that fades quickly on death.*

Billfish

hese are the glamour fish of warmer waters, and at least one of the species is available to anglers in most coastal states. The Billfish Fishery Management Plan created by the Fishery Management Councils covering the Atlantic, Gulf of Mexico and Caribbean now protects all of the billfish except swordfish from commercial exploitation with the exception of a small native handline fishery for marlin in Puerto Rico. This precedent reserves these fish for sport fishing purposes and prohibits their sale.

ATLANTIC SAILFISH (*Istiophorus platypterus*)

■ **RANGE**: Atlantic coast of Florida and north to Virginia; Gulf of Mexico.

■ **WEIGHT**: Average 30–50 pounds, up to over 125 pounds.

By far the most abundant of the billfish, the Atlantic sailfish is usually found close to shore – unlike most billfish. The Gulf Stream runs just a few miles offshore in southeast Florida, and sailfish frequent the drop-off of the reef rather than the depths favored by marlin, spearfish and swordfish. There's no mistaking the sailfish for anything else due to the long, sail-like dorsal fin. This fast-growing and very short-lived species tends to group in certain feeding areas, and the individuals may even work together to "ball the bait" (concentrate it in an ever-smaller circle) during the peak winter migratory period off Florida's Gold Coast. Most sailfish are taken by trolling with either dead bait (balao, small mullet, strip baits, etc.) or live balao, pilchards, blue runners or goggle eyes. They are excellent sport on light tackle.

PACIFIC SAILFISH

■ **RANGE**: Pacific coast, north to Mexico and Baja California.

■ **WEIGHT**: Average 100 pounds and up to over 200 pounds.

Equally as spectacular in aeriel acrobatics as the Atlantic species, the Pacific sailfish is not regarded as highly as a fighting fish on a pound-for-pound basis.

WHITE MARLIN (*Tetrapturus albidus*)

■ **RANGE**: Atlantic coast north to Cape Cod; Gulf of Mexico.

■ **WEIGHT**: Average 40–60 pounds, up to almost 200 pounds.

White marlin can be readily separated from the much larger blue marlin by the rounded, rather than pointed, tips of the pectoral fins and both the first dorsal and first anal fins. Many anglers regard the white as the best fighter among the marlins on a pound-for-pound basis. They are certainly an excellent fish on light tackle (no more than 30-pound) and usually do a lot of jumping. In the Gulf, whites tend to be found well offshore in the Loop Current and although the best fishing to the north is usually in offshore waters, white marlin frequently populate areas much closer to shore. Trolling is the normal method of catching them, with both bait (usually balao, mullet or eels) and high-speed lures being effective.

BLUE MARLIN (*Makaira nigricans*)

■ **RANGE**: Atlantic – north to Massachusetts; Gulf of Mexico. Pacific – from Mexico south; Hawaii.

■ **WEIGHT**: Average 200–500 pounds, up to 2000 pounds.

The Pacific and Atlantic blue marlin are probably the same species or subspecies, but the IGFA does maintain separate record classifications for them. Mainly taken in offshore waters, some are caught in waters within 20 miles or so of shore where the Gulf Stream approaches shore in southeast Florida and at Cape Hatteras. For anglers from Virginia north, the blue marlin is basically a canyon fish, but some of the very

largest blues have been caught in those far-offshore waters of New Jersey and New York, where the state records are well over the 1000-pound mark. Blues can be distinguished from whites by the pointed, rather than rounded, dorsal, pectoral and anal fins.

Pacific blues can be separated from the similarly sized black marlin by the fact that their pectoral fins are never rigid, and can be folded completely flat against the sides even in death. This oceanic wanderer is considered to be one of the finest game fish as well as a spectacular leaper. Almost all are taken by trolling high-speed lures or dead baits such as mullet, balao, Spanish mackerel, bonefish and smaller members of the tuna family. Live baiting is very effective, with small tunas and dolphin caught on the spot being the usual offerings.

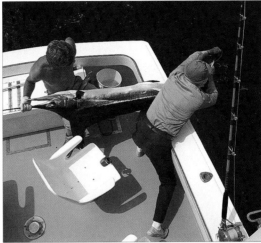

LEFT *The line is untangled from a white marlin's tail before its release off the North Carolina coast.*

FAR LEFT *The pectoral fin of the black marlin is rigid, whereas the similar-looking blue has a pectoral that will fold flat against its body.*

BLACK MARLIN (*Makaira indica*)

■ **RANGE:** Pacific coast from Baja California south to Peru; Hawaii.
■ **WEIGHT:** Average 200–500 pounds, up to 2000 pounds.
The sure means of distinguishing a black marlin from a blue involves the rigid pectoral fins which cannot be folded back against the body without breaking the joints. In the case of both black and blue marlins, almost all specimens exceeding 300 pounds will be females.

STRIPED MARLIN (*Tetrapturus audax*)

■ **RANGE:** Eastern Pacific from California south to Peru; also Hawaii.
■ **WEIGHT:** Average 100–200 pounds, up to 500 pounds in W. Pacific.
Striped marlin are the most common Pacific marlin. Whereas color isn't a very good guide to identifying blue and black marlin, the striped marlin can't be mistaken due to the blue or lavender stripes on the sides and blue spots on the fins – all of which are still prominent after death. The sides are also very compressed as compared to the bulky appearance of the blue and black, and the pointed first dorsal fin is higher than in the other marlin. Striped marlin are surface fish that are usually spotted and baited, rather than being raised by blind trolling. They may be caught on dead balao, mullet, flying fish and other relatively small baits, but live baits of a similar size, such as mackerels, jacks and even bottom fish, are most effective.

BELOW *A fine broadbill swordfish.*

SWORDFISH (*Xiphias gladius*)

RANGE: Pacific and Atlantic.

WEIGHT: Average 100–500 pounds, perhaps up to 2000 pounds.

Swordfish are distributed worldwide in both temperate and tropical waters. Broadbills are distinguished from other billfish by the very long, wide, smooth and flattened sword. They also lack ventral fins, and the adults have no scales. This is by far the best-eating of the billfish, and the object of an intense worldwide commercial fishery that has severely depleted its numbers. Previously a common sight on the surface in the North Atlantic, the swordfish is now taken primarily on lines fished in offshore depths at night. However, surfacing swordfish are still common off California where they can be taken in the traditional manner of trolling a bait in front of them and then letting it drop in free-spool in the hope that the dozing swordfish will pick it up. Most veteran swordfish anglers estimate that only about one-in-ten surfacing swords will hit, and many of those are lost due to hooks pulling out of their soft mouth. Squid is the most popular bait, though any reasonably sized fish will also work.

LONGBILL SPEARFISH (*Tetrapturus pfluegeri*)

RANGE: Atlantic coast north to New Jersey; Gulf of Mexico.

WEIGHT: Average 30–40 pounds, up to 100 pounds.

Spearfish are the most unusual of billfish. They tend to live further offshore, and are rarely caught by sport fishermen. These fish have very short bills and a slender body with a pointed first dorsal fin that looks like a cross between that of a marlin and a sailfish. The longbill spearfish has a bill about twice as long as its lower jaw. Spearfish are short-lived and are so uncommon that they are caught only on an incidental basis by anglers seeking other billfish.

Tunas

While the question of which species is the greatest game fish can be the source of endless argument, there is no doubt in my mind that members of the tuna family have the clear upper hand. While tunas do not jump when hooked, they are the most powerful of all fish – and among the fastest. According to the IGFA, bluefin tuna have been clocked at speeds up to 43.4 mph in bursts of 10 to 20 seconds duration. While huge marlin are often caught on very light lines, tuna records on similar lines remain very low. For example, the black marlin record on 20-pound line stands at 1051 pounds, while the bluefin tuna mark in the same line class was only 119 pounds! Very rarely does a tuna come in easily. One reason for the exceptional power of the tunas is the fact that they aren't completely cold-blooded: their body temperature can be as much as 18 degrees Fahrenheit higher than the surrounding water. It has been estimated that such a rise in body temperature effectively triples the power and response of a muscle mass. Due to the heat built up in a hooked tuna's body, it's important to bleed it upon capture and keep it cool to assure fine eating quality.

LEFT A giant tuna goes up on the gin pole off Montauk, New York.

▓ BLUEFIN TUNA (*Thunnus thynnus*) ▓

■ **RANGE:** North Atlantic to Gulf of Mexico; temperate Pacific waters.

■ **WEIGHT:** School – 10–135 pounds; medium – 135–315 pounds; giant – 315–2000 pounds.

This species is the giant of the tuna family, growing to a ton or more. Tuna fishing as a sport started off southern California in 1898, when a bluefin of 183 pounds was caught off the Catalina Islands. However, the glory days of Pacific bluefin fishing are over, a victim of intense commercial fishing. Prior to the 1960s, bluefin tuna were hardly exploited at all along the Atlantic Coast of the United States, but by the mid-1970s, the bluefin population had dropped to about 10% of what it had been. Rigid management measures have been instituted since then by the federal government, in cooperation with Canada and Japan. The basic problem with the giant tuna is its great value as a fresh food fish in Japan. Prices as high as $20 a pound (headed and gutted) were paid to American longliners for prime giants during the winter of 1988. Over the years, giant tuna feeding grounds have shifted considerably. For instance, the Soldier's Rip area off Wedgeport, Nova Scotia, that once drew anglers from all over the world died out many years ago – but Prince Edward Island and the Canso Causeway area of Nova Scotia (in the fall) have been good bets for the largest giants since the 1970s.

Bluefins can easily be confused with yellowfins and bigeyes in smaller sizes. The bluefin is distinguished by its short pectoral fins and the highest gill raker count of any tuna – 34 to 43 on the first arch. The sure distinguishing feature in relation to the yellowfin is the striated liver – as compared to the yellowfin's smooth liver. Smaller bluefins, known as school tuna, are usually taken by high-speed trolling with relatively actionless lures such as feathers or cedar jigs, or by chunking. Mediums and giants are also taken by the chunking technique (using cut bait as chum) or by slow trolling with daisy chains or spreader bars armed with real or soft plastic mackerel or squid.

ABOVE Moving a giant tuna is no easy matter, as Captains Billy and Jay De Noia find while fishing on Stellwagen Bank off Gloucester, Massachusetts.

TOP *This bigeye tuna was trolled in Hudson Canyon.*

BELOW *The long pectoral fin of the albacore separates it immediately from all other tunas.*

▓ YELLOWFIN TUNA (*Thunnus albacares*) ▓

■ **RANGE:** Atlantic coast from Florida to Cape Cod; Gulf of Mexico. Pacific coast off Baja California, Mexico and occasionally off S. California.

■ **WEIGHT:** Average 50–200 pounds, up to 400 pounds.

This is the most colorful of the tunas, and all the fins and finlets are golden yellow. Large yellowfins often have overextended second dorsal and anal fins. Such specimens used to be referred to as Allisons, but biologists now maintain that they are one and the same species. Dead yellowfins may look similar to bluefins except for the longer pectoral fins – though the smooth liver is the sure identification.

This excellent eating fish is favored by commercial fishermen for canning. Most are caught commercially by purse seining, but many fall to sportsmen using chunking and high speed trolling techniques. While yellowfins tend to stay well offshore in deep waters throughout most of their range, they are taken not far off the reef at Key West and in the Gulf Stream where it runs only about 20 miles offshore at Cape Hatteras. Surprisingly, yellowfins also started populating relatively shallow waters (80 to 140 feet) from northern New Jersey to Block Island in the mid-1980s, and anglers there made large catches (primarily by chunking) of 50- to 150-pound yellowfins in July and August only 10 to 25 miles from shore.

▓ BIGEYE TUNA (*Thunnus obesus*) ▓

■ **RANGE:** Atlantic coast canyons; Pacific coast south from California.

■ **WEIGHT:** Average 100 pounds plus, up to 400 pounds.

The bigeye tuna is a deepwater fish that favors cooler waters, and is most abundant in the northern canyons from Toms and Hudson to Block and Atlantis. Though they frequently respond to high-speed trolling lures, night chunking is also effective – and many are taken on diamond jigs. The Japanese regard the bigeye as a close second choice to giant bluefins as a fresh fish, making the larger specimens quite valuable.

▓ ALBACORE (*Thunnus alalunga*) ▓

■ **RANGE:** Atlantic and Pacific coasts.

■ **WEIGHT:** Average 30–60 pounds, up to 100 pounds.

An important game and food fish also known as longfin, this tuna is immediately identified by its very long pectoral fins that reach to a point beyond the anal fin. Chunking and trolling are the usual methods for fishing in the Atlantic. In the Pacific, marine scientists can usually predict just about when albacore will move within range each summer – depending on currents and water temperatures – but the fishery varies greatly from year-to-year. Whereas the Atlantic longfins are rarely line-shy and readily hit dead baits in a chum line, the Pacific fish tend to be very line-shy and want live anchovies that must be cast to them on relatively light tackle. Albacore are sought after by commercial trollers since they are the most valuable tuna for canning – and the only one which can be labeled "white meat tuna."

LEFT A yellowfin tuna caught off Montauk, New York.

TOP *The skipjack tuna is readily identified by the "pajama pants" stripes on the lower portion of its body.*

ABOVE *The little tunny is a fine inshore game fish which is mistakenly called "bonito" in southern areas.*

▮ BLACKFIN TUNA (*Thunnus atlanticus*) ▮

■ **RANGE**: Atlantic coast from Florida to North Carolina.
■ **WEIGHT**: Average 10–25 pounds, up to 50 pounds.
The finlets of these small schooling fish are uniformly dark, without any of the yellow coloration present in other tunas. They are most abundant off the reef at Key West and on the hump off Islamorada. Trolling with bait or lures is effective, but the deadliest method involves chumming with live pilchards.

▮ SKIPJACK TUNA (*Euthynnus pelamis*) ▮

■ **RANGE**: Atlantic coast, from Cape Cod south.
■ **WEIGHT**: Average 5–15 pounds, up to 50 pounds.
Probably the most widely distributed and prolific member of the tuna tribe, they range throughout tropical and subtropical seas, and in the Atlantic are found from Cape Cod to Argentina. Skipjacks are easily identified by the "pajama pants" stripes on the belly and the lack of markings on the back. They travel in huge schools and are heavily exploited by purse seiners for lower-grade canned tuna and cat food. Most are taken by anglers when they're trolling for larger tunas with heavy tackle, but they are fine sport when light tackle is used. Skipjacks will hit many types of lures and trolled baits, but feathers are hard to beat when they are the target species.

▮ LITTLE TUNNY (*Euthynnus alletteratus*) ▮

■ **RANGE**: Atlantic.
■ **WEIGHT**: Average 5–15 pounds, up to 30 pounds.
Readily identified by the scattering of dark spots between the pectoral and ventral fins, little tunny also sport wavy "worm-like" markings on the back. Unlike most other tunas, they regularly feed close to shore – even invading the surf at times. The little tunny has a poor name for a great game fish, but the local names are even worse: in the Mid-Atlantic it's called false albacore, while in Florida and the Gulf it's referred to as bonito, which is another species. Little tunny are favorites of inshore anglers, since they provide a terrific first run on light tackle and never give up. Unfortunately, that gameness often results in their death before it's possible to release them. Among all the tunas, the little tunny is the poorest on the table and the best bet is to release this great warrior which is regularly caught by anglers trolling for other species. In Florida, the little tunny is prized primarily for the strip baits that can be cut from its belly.

▮ ATLANTIC BONITO (*Sarda sarda*) ▮

■ **RANGE**: Atlantic coast, primarily from New Jersey to southern New England.
■ **WEIGHT**: Average 3–7 pounds, up to 20 pounds.
Bonito are closely related to the tunas, and often mix with them. They differ in appearance from tuna in that they have stripes on the back rather than the belly, their bodies are slimmer, and the mouth is full of tiny, sharp teeth. The Atlantic bonito is very popular with

anglers due to its fighting qualities and edibility. Lures must be trolled or retrieved at relatively high speeds for these fish, and they also are attracted to chum lines.

Pacific bonito (*Sarda chiliensis*) range north to California. These schooling fish (reaching up to 20 pounds) are a popular party boat quarry in southern California. Like the Atlantic species, they have light-colored flesh and are very good eating.

Sharks

These ancient creatures have survived almost unchanged, and continue to hold their own in waters throughout the world. Little was known about them until recently, but tagging, primarily by volunteer sportsmen, has established migratory patterns and given an indication of growth rates. Sharks are slow-growing, long-lived fish with a low reproductive capacity. Wherever intense commercial fisheries have established, their numbers have been quickly diminished to the point where the venture was no longer practical. Unfortunately, that pressure is building steadily as shark meat has become accepted as table fare. Without management of the resource, it's unlikely that we'll enjoy a shark fishery in the future such as was available when sportfishing for them was popularized during the post-World War II period. For eating purposes, sharks should be bled and gutted as soon as possible – preferably at sea.

BELOW This 150-pound mako was caught off Margate, New Jersey.

▮ SHORTFIN MAKO SHARK (*Isurus oxyrinchus*) ▮
■ **RANGE:** Worldwide in warm temperate and tropical seas. Atlantic – Florida to Cape Cod; Gulf of Mexico. Pacific – California south.
■ **WEIGHT:** Average 50–200 pounds, up to 1000 pounds.
This is the most prized of all sharks, a true game fish capable of blistering runs and the most spectacular leaps of all the big game fish. The mako is an excellent eating fish with meat similar in looks and taste to the very expensive swordfish. This very popular species is taken on baits drifted in chum lines off the Mid-Atlantic and California. The mako often moves into depths of 20 fathoms or less in the Mid-Atlantic.

The very similar **longfin mako** (*Isurus paucus*) is a deepwater species of the Atlantic and Gulf of Mexico which is rarely encountered by anglers. Also closely related (in the mackerel shark family, Lamnidae) is the **porbeagle** (*Lamna nasus*), a fine sport and food species of the North Atlantic which was long ago decimated by longlining.

▮ WHITE SHARK (*Carcharodon carcharias*) ▮
■ **RANGE:** Atlantic coast, primarily from New Jersey to Maine; Pacific coast, especially off San Francisco.
■ **WEIGHT:** Up to several tons.
The other prominent member of this family is the white shark – better-known to most as the "man-eater." This shark grows to several

RIGHT *The long tail of the thresher distinguishes it from all other sharks.*

tons, and one of 3,427 pounds was caught on rod-and-reel (though not officially recognized by the IGFA) in 1986. The white is as abundant in U.S. waters as anywhere – but still a very rare catch.

▮ BLUE SHARK (*Prionace glauca*) ▮
■ **RANGE:** Atlantic coast, particularly New Jersey to Maine; Pacific coast, especially off California.
■ **WEIGHT:** Pacific – average under 100 pounds; Atlantic – average 50–200 pounds, up to over 400 pounds.
Very widely distributed in cool temperate seas, the blue shark may be the most abundant of the large sharks which move inshore at times. Though recognized as a game fish by the IGFA, blue sharks often put up relatively little fight. They are not at all line shy, and can usually be chummed right to the boat where any type of light tackle can be used to catch them. These "dumb" sharks frequently return to hit again after release. Blue sharks have watery meat that few anglers enjoy and are therefore usually released.

▮ LONGTAIL THRESHER (*Alopias vulpinus*) ▮
■ **RANGE:** Atlantic coast, primarily from New Jersey to Block Island; Pacific Coast, especially off southern California.
■ **WEIGHT:** Average 200–500 pounds, up to 800 pounds.
Thresher sharks are well-distributed throughout the world and this is the most common sub-species, found worldwide in warm to cool temperate zones. It boasts an upper lobe of the tail which is longer than the rest of the body. The high price paid for their flesh has resulted in a serious decline in numbers off California, once their most common location.

▮ TIGER SHARK (*Galeocerdo cuvieri*) ▮
■ **RANGE:** Atlantic coast, Florida to Cape Cod.
■ **WEIGHT:** Up to 2000 pounds.
The tiger shark also occurs worldwide, but in tropical and warmer temperate seas. Tigers are very large, but lazy and can be easily overpowered on heavy tackle.

▮ HAMMERHEAD SHARK – FAMILY SPHYRNIDAE ▮
■ **RANGE:** Atlantic, Gulf and Pacific coasts.
■ **SIZE:** Varies according to species.
Hammerhead sharks are immediately identified by their unique head in which the eyes are located at the ends of two thin protrusions resembling a hammer. They have a worldwide distribution covered by several species. Most common is the **smooth hammerhead** (*Sphyrna zygaena*), which grows to 14 feet and is frequently found in shallow waters. The **great hammerhead** (*Sphyrna mokarran*) grows to 20 feet, and the **scalloped hammerhead** (*Sphyrna lewini*) reaches 10 feet. The great hammerhead has a T-shaped head which is notched in the center, while the smooth hammerhead's head is rounded and unnotched, and the scalloped hammerhead is rounded and notched. A similar very

TOP *The distinctive shape of the hammerhead cannot be confused with any other shark.*

ABOVE *Blue sharks frequently swim right to boatside and stay there, waiting to be caught.*

BELOW Sherilynn Ristori with a dolphin trolled off Fort Pierce, Florida. This small specimen is a female, identified by the rounded head.

small member of this family is the **bonnethead** (*Sphyrna tiburo*), a shallow water species (common in the Florida Keys) with a very short-lobed, shovel-shaped head. Hammerheads look like lazy sharks when seen cruising on the surface, but they are actually good game fish – and can be quite fussy. It's not unusual for hammerheads to swim around in chum slicks but refuse to hit.

▌ SANDBAR SHARK (*Carcharhinus milberti*) ▌
▌ DUSKY SHARK (*Carcharhinus obscurus*) ▌

■**RANGE:** Atlantic coast, Florida to Cape Cod; Gulf of Mexico.
■**WEIGHT:** Sandbar – average 30–100 pounds, up to 200 pounds; dusky – to over 600 pounds.

Among the many sharks not listed as game fish by the IGFA, but of interest to anglers, are the very similar sandbar and dusky sharks. The sandbar is distinguished from the bigger dusky by its larger first dorsal that is also further forward in relation to the pectoral fins. Sandbars are better known as brown sharks in the Mid-Atlantic states, where the females enter bays to give birth. This is the most common shark of inshore waters. The dusky is a far less abundant bottom feeder and found in the same offshore areas frequented by the sandbar.

LEFT Legendary shark expert Captain Frank Mundus with the biggest fish ever caught on rod-and-reel – a 3427-pound white shark taken off Montauk in 1986. The catch wasn't recognized by the IGFA as it was caught while feeding off a dead whale.

BELOW Sandbar (brown) sharks are the most common inshore shark found along the Atlantic and Gulf coasts.

▮ BLACKTIP SHARK (*Carcharhinus limbatus*) ▮
▮ SPINNER SHARK (*Carcharhinus brevipinna*) ▮

■ RANGE: Atlantic Coast from N. Carolina to Florida; Gulf of Mexico.
■ WEIGHT: Average under 100 pounds, up to 300 pounds.
The blacktip and spinner are both great sport on light tackle, frequently hitting plugs and jigs cast very close to their heads.

Dolphin
(*Coryphaena hippurus*)

■ RANGE: Atlantic Coast, particularly southeast Florida and N. Carolina, but also north to Cape Cod; Gulf of Mexico; Hawaii.
■ WEIGHT: From 1–3 pounds to maximum of 100 pounds.
This fish is one of the most widely distributed species of tropical and warm temperate seas throughout the world. Though basically an open ocean fish, the dolphin does move into shallower waters on occasion. There is no mistaking it for any other species, though the golden colors fade to gray when the fish dies. It's also possible to immediately separate the sexes in this fish: males have high, vertical foreheads, while females' heads are rounded.

Trolling with baits (particularly balao) and lures is the usual method for catching these fish, but schools can also be chummed to the boat and taken on small jigs or pieces of bait. By keeping a hooked dolphin in the water at all times, the school will usually stay with the boat. Dolphin are famed for their association with floating objects. Weed lines and even the smallest boards found in warm (over 70 degrees Fahrenheit), clean offshore waters should always be investigated. The dolphin is truly one of the great game fish, as it can attain speeds of up to about 50 mph, provides frequent and spectacular jumps – and then prolongs the fight by utilizing its broad sides to keep the rod doubled over at boatside. Yet, as hard as they fight, dolphin still have plenty in reserve when they're gaffed. Throw big ones immediately into the fish box and sit on the lid in order to prevent damage to both the boat and crew. Dolphin, called mahi-mahi in Hawaii and dorado in Latin America, are among the very best eating fish in the oceans – though the soft and delicate meat doesn't maintain its quality unless the fish is kept cool.

Jacks

The Carangidae family rivals the tunas in fighting quality. Most members of the family combine toughness with speed and a "never say die" attitude. There are so many species involved (about 140) that there are few characteristics common to all of these warm-water fish except a deeply-forked caudal fin. Only the most prominent will be noted here.

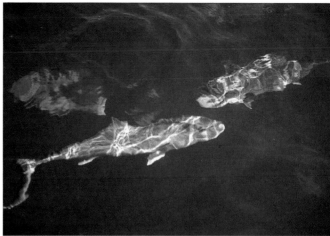

LEFT *A typical amberjack from deepwater wrecks on the Atlantic side of Key West. Notice the "fighting" stripe running through the eye.*

ABOVE *Amberjack can often be tempted right to the surface over shallower wrecks by using a live bait as a decoy or by stirring them up with a popping plug. These amberjack were found on the 12 Mile Wreck off Carolina Beach, North Carolina.*

AMBERJACK (*Seriola dumerili*)

RANGE: Atlantic Coast, around Florida Keys in winter, and north to North Carolina and Virginia in summer; juveniles to New York; Gulf of Mexico.

WEIGHT: Average 30–50 pounds and up to over 150 pounds.

Amberjack are found almost worldwide in tropical and warm temperate waters. The largest of the jacks can be found in many habitats, but are most closely associated with wrecks, reefs and offshore buoys or oil rigs. It's an extremely strong fish which has worn out many an angler, particularly when hooked in deep water. Amberjack will rarely pass up a live bait fish, but also readily hit jigs in deep water, and, when near the surface, can usually be excited into violent strikes by fast-moving popping plugs. At such times the olive-colored "fighting" stripe running from the mouth through the eye and almost to the first dorsal fin "lights up." These fish are edible, but usually have worms in the meat which discourages consumption. Releasing them is generally the best bet. A similar **Pacific amberjack** (*Seriola colburni*) ranging from Baja California to Peru, can weigh over 100 pounds.

RIGHT *The African pompano is even more colorful when young, as it then features long filaments extending from the dorsal and anal fins.*

ABOVE *Yellowtail are closely related to the amberjack, and are one of the most popular species in southern California.*

▮ YELLOWTAIL (*Seriola lalandei*) ▮

■**RANGE:** Pacific coast, off southern California and Baja California.

■**WEIGHT:** Average 5–20 pounds, up to 80 pounds.

The body shape of the yellowtail is like that of the amberjack, but a light lemon-yellow stripe runs along the median line, and the tail is yellow. Live bait is the most common temptation offered to these major sport fish, but they also readily take many types of lures.

▮ JACK CREVALLE (*Caranx hippos*) ▮

■**RANGE:** Atlantic coast off Florida and up to North Carolina; Gulf of Mexico.

■**WEIGHT:** Average 8–15 pounds, and up to 50 pounds or more.

This inshore species is a very tough customer, found from the reef into shallow bay waters. The jack crevalle is a voracious predator, regularly chasing schools of mullet almost too large for them to swallow. They use their broad sides to prolong the fight, which can last a long time if light tackle is employed. Though an outstanding fighting fish, the jack crevalle has dark meat of relatively poor quality and is usually released by American anglers. The species can quickly be distinguished from other jacks by the dark spot on the pectoral fin and the gill cover.

▮ HORSE-EYE JACK (*Caranx latus*) ▮

■**RANGE:** Particularly around Bahamas.

■**WEIGHT:** Average 8–15 pounds, and up to 30 pounds.

The horse-eye jack tends to feed at night, has a rather large eye and, unlike the jack crevalle, no black spot on the pectoral fin. It also has dark, poor-quality meat and is associated with ciguatera poisoning.

AFRICAN POMPANO (*Alectis ciliaris*)

■**RANGE:** Southeast Florida coast.

■**WEIGHT:** Average 10–30 pounds, up to 50 pounds.

This species has a jack-like profile as an adult, but when young has the roundish appearance of the pompano with the addition of four to six long, beautiful filaments streaming from the dorsal and anal fins. As the African pompano grows, the filaments disappear and the body shape changes – though the silver sides remain. This fine fighting fish frequents reefs and wrecks in southeast Florida, but is never abundant.

POMPANO (*Trachinotus carolinus*)

■**RANGE:** Atlantic coast, from Florida up to North Carolina (in summer); Gulf of Mexico.

■**WEIGHT:** Average 1–5 pounds and up to 8 pounds.

The pompanos belong to the Carangidae family, and fight as well as the other jacks. This is one of the most highly esteemed eating fish in the world, and also a fine game fish that will hit small jigs in shallow waters. It is taken in large numbers by Florida surfcasters who use long rods to cast sand fleas to the outer bar.

PERMIT (*Trachinotus falcatus*)

■**RANGE:** Southern Florida coasts.

■**WEIGHT:** Average 5–25 pounds, up to 60 pounds.

Very similar in appearance, but growing to much greater sizes is the permit – the largest of the pompanos. These shallow-water fish frequent Florida Keys flats and Gulf wrecks in southwest Florida. The silvery permit is the greatest challenge for the light-tackle flats angler who must flip a live crab to the wary fish. Catching permit on a fly rod is particularly difficult, and few have succeeded in tempting them. Though an excellent eating fish, most permit not desired for mounting are usually released.

Mackerel

These swift, slim fish are members of the Scombridae family along with the tunas and bonitos. All are noted for the speed they can develop in short bursts, though none has the endurance of the tunas. Like the tunas, some mackerels clear the water when pursuing bait and yet very rarely jump when hooked.

ATLANTIC MACKEREL (*Scomber scrombrus*)

■**RANGE:** North Atlantic.

■**WEIGHT:** Average 1–3 pounds and up to 8 pounds.

The mackerel taken in the greatest quantities is the Atlantic mackerel of northern waters on both sides of that ocean. Each spring, vast schools of these fish (often called Boston mackerel) start moving inshore off Virginia and Maryland. Then they quickly swim up the coast to Delaware and southern New Jersey by around April 1. Within a couple of weeks, schools can be expected in the Metropolitan New

ABOVE *Pompano, such as these caught around oil rigs off the Louisiana coast, are both great game fish and one of the most highly desired food fishes in the world.*

*A big king mackerel,
caught at an oil rig off the
Louisiana coast.*

York area, and they spread east from there. The big runs last only two weeks to a month, but anglers often catch over 100 a day while jigging from party boats fishing just a few miles to 20 miles or so offshore. A separate stock of mackerel populates areas from Cape Cod north into the Canadian Maritime Provinces, and provides a solid spring through fall fishery. Mackerel can be caught in many ways, but the usual method involves three or more tiny tubes or feathers rigged on small hooks along a leader with a diamond jig at the end. This rig is dropped to the level of the fish, and is often loaded up before the fisherman can begin retrieving it. They make excellent cut baits for many species, and are sought after as live baits for trophy striped bass by New England anglers. Since they are a cyclical species, Atlantic mackerel runs can vary greatly from year-to-year.

KING MACKEREL (*Scomberomorus cavalla*)

■ **RANGE:** Atlantic coast from Florida to Virginia; Gulf of Mexico.
■ **WEIGHT:** Average 5–30 pounds, up to over 90 pounds.
Kingfish (the common name throughout the species normal range) tend to range along the reef and often move within range of anglers fishing off ocean piers – but don't normally enter bay waters. Great numbers of 5- to 15-pound kings used to be taken off southeast Florida in the winter and spring, off Texas in the summer and North Carolina in the fall – but overfishing resulted in a population crash and strict regulations on both sport and commercial catches. This fine game fish

is often spotted making long, high leaps after bait fish or onto a trolled lure. In addition to trolling, live baiting is very effective – but it's important to use a wire leader with a "stinger" hook toward the rear of the bait. The king has no spots (except when very young), and there's a sharp dip in the lateral line under the second dorsal fin. It is an excellent eating fish which is usually cut in steaks.

▓ SPANISH MACKEREL (*Scomberomorus maculatus*) ▓
▓ CERO MACKEREL (*Scomberomorus regalis*) ▓

■ **RANGE:** Spanish – Atlantic coast from Florida to Virginia; Gulf of Mexico. Cero – Gulf Stream waters.

■ **WEIGHT:** Spanish – average 1–5 pounds, up to 15 pounds. Cero – up to 20 pounds or more.

Both species are closely related to the king mackerel, though much smaller. The Spanish is distinguishable by bronze or yellow spots and no stripes on the sides, and this schooling fish is a particularly easy target for netters, though its numbers have been reduced to the point where strict quotas and seasons had to be instituted. A fine eating fish and great light-tackle sport, it will hit just about any lure that can be moved at a high rate of speed. Like the king and cero, they have sharp teeth – necessitating the use of wire or Steelon leaders. Ceros are larger mackerel that resemble both the king and Spanish mackerel, but are identified by spots that are elongated rather than round and arranged in distinct rows.

BELOW Captain Bob Wilder hoses down the deck of his Double T from Point Pleasant, New Jersey, since fast action in a school of Atlantic mackerel prevented stowing the catch below decks.

RIGHT Bluefish are crowd pleasers in the Mid-Atlantic and Northeast.

▮ WAHOO (*Acanthocybium solanderi*) ▮

■ **RANGE:** Pacific coast – north to Baja California. Atlantic coast – Florida to Cape Cod, in Gulf Stream waters and northern canyons; Gulf of Mexico.

■ **WEIGHT:** Average 20–60 pounds, up to 150 pounds or more.

The most desirable of the mackerels is the wahoo, an oceanic wanderer that usually swims alone or in very small groups. It may be the fastest fish in the world and is also among the very best eating fish. Most are caught by trolling, and wire line is used effectively in the Bahamas to catch them when they're not hitting on the surface. Wahoo have very sharp teeth, and tend to slice baits in half – often with such speed and accuracy that the line isn't even pulled from the outrigger. Naturally, wire leaders are a must. The wahoo is easily identified by the bright blue or black vertical bands flowing down the sides.

Bluefish
(Pomatomus saltatrix)

■ **RANGE:** Atlantic coast from Maine to Florida, also Gulf of Mexico.

■ **WEIGHT:** Average 2–15 pounds, up to about 40 pounds.

This is, by far, the most important saltwater recreational fish in the U.S., despite the fact that it isn't even found on the West Coast. The bluefish is the sole member of the family Pomatomidae, and is widely distributed throughout temperate to tropical waters worldwide – though both size and abundance may vary greatly. Bluefish have everything going for them as game fish. They are relatively large, fight hard, jump, take all manner of lures and baits, frequent inshore waters – and are good to eat. They are also available to surf, pier and bay fishermen just as they are to those who fish offshore – and there's no need to journey to remote areas. Indeed, anglers often curse bluefish because they can't fish through them to catch striped bass, weakfish, sharks or bluefin tuna. These voracious fish are frequently referred to as "choppers," due to their propensity to chop up bait fish with their sharp teeth and then pick up the leftovers.

Though numerous fishermen have scars to attest to those teeth, most lures are fished on mono leaders since the blue tends to hit from behind and such lures as diamond jigs, tubes and plugs don't work well on wire leaders. The most efficient bluefish lure is the umbrella rig, a usually four-armed wire contraption from which tube lures are fished. This lure, fished deep with wire line, imitates a school of sand eels (at present the primary forage fish in the Northeast), and multiple catches are common. For sport, popping plugs are the best bet as bluefish will provide smashing strikes when they're feeding near the surface. Bluefish feed day and night after they move inshore and migrate north each spring, and are reluctant to leave in the fall. Even with water temperatures dropping under 50 degrees Fahrenheit, bluefish often remain abundant off New York and New Jersey into early December. Though a good eating fish when cleaned promptly and kept cool, bluefish don't freeze well. It's that fact which has so far prevented development of a foreign market and kept the blue a relatively inexpensive fresh fish species of limited interest to commercial fishermen.

Striped Bass
(Morone saxatilis)

■ **RANGE:** Atlantic coast, from Nova Scotia to Florida; Gulf of Mexico. Pacific coast, from San Francisco to Oregon.

■ **WEIGHT:** Average 5–25 pounds, up to 90 pounds. 125 pounds recorded in 19th century.

Known as rockfish from Chesapeake Bay south, this is probably the most esteemed and sought-after inshore saltwater game fish and is found along the entire East Coast. The migratory striped bass run from North Carolina to Maine involves anadromous stripers who live in the bays and ocean from spring through fall, but return to bay wintering grounds and spawn in rivers during early spring. The populations in Canada and south of Hatteras are considered to be non-migratory.

ABOVE *These school striped bass (called rock from Delaware south) were plugged in the evening from Cape Fear River in the southern portion of North Carolina. Striped bass found below Cape Hatteras rarely, if ever, leave the river systems they reside in.*

Striped bass require rivers with long enough stretches of fresh water to keep their eggs floating for two days. Only a few rivers meet that criteria, and the major spawning areas flow into Chesapeake Bay. The Hudson River is the northernmost spawning area, and normally contributes much of the stock for the Metropolitan New York region. An unexplained drop in productivity since 1970 has resulted in the imposition of strict regulations. Striped bass on the West Coast are the result of a transplant effort that started with 107 small bass shipped by train from the Navesink River in New Jersey to the Carquinez Straits near San Francisco in 1879. Another 300 from New Jersey's Shrewsbury River were released in Suisun Bay, California, in 1882. From those small beginnings came the big western sportfishery. In order to protect this valuable resource, California made it a game fish in 1936.

Striped bass live to 20 years or more and are good fighters which frequent inshore waters and take a wide variety of lures and baits, day and night. They're also a very good eating fish, a fact which contributes to the great pressure on the species.

Drum

The Sciaenidae family includes the drums, weakfish and croakers. Though there is a great deal of variety within the family, the most common denominator is the ability to produce sound by vibrating a muscle near the swim bladder. In some species, only the male can create this noise. All are good eating fish.

Important members of this family to be mentioned briefly include the **Atlantic croaker** (*Micropogonias undulatus*), which is a small but important food and sport species of the Chesapeake Bay area when the cycle is "up," and the **spot** (*Leiostomus xanthurus*), a tiny panfish of that region which rarely reaches a pound but is also an important forage fish for larger species. A live spot is hard to beat as a bait for a trophy weakfish. The **northern kingfish** *Menticirrhus saxatilis*) is a small but colorful species of the Mid-Atlantic surf that sports an underslung mouth and makes delicious eating. There are similar southern and gulf kingfish plus the California **corbina** (*Menticirrhus undulatus*) – an even more important surf species.

RED DRUM (*Sciaenops ocellatus*)

RANGE: Atlantic coast from Florida to Virginia, and Gulf Coast from Florida to Texas.
WEIGHT: Average 5–50 pounds, up to 100 pounds.
This is the greatest game fish of the family. Formerly known as channel bass, and simply called redfish in the south, the red drum is a large fish of inshore waters and is famed for its fighting qualities – though it does not jump. Redfish are especially important to anglers fishing with light tackle in shallow inshore waters along the Gulf Coast. Puppy drum strike readily at jigs tipped with shrimp and on small spoons, while the larger fish are taken primarily on bait. Red drum have a copper coloration and there is always at least one black spot about the size of an eye at the base of the tail fin.

OPPOSITE *Captain Bob Rocchetta with his 76-pound striped bass caught on a live eel off Montauk Point in 1981 during an eclipse of the moon. This record striper broke a mark that had stood for seven decades. Ironically, it was beaten by a 78½-pounder from Atlantic City, New Jersey, the very next year, but continued as the IGFA 50-pound line class record.*

TOP *Black drum are not the greatest fighting fish, but they do grow big. This was just an average-sized specimen from Delaware Bay.*

ABOVE *This big red drum (channel bass) was caught at night on a flat in Pamlico Sound, North Carolina.*

▮ BLACK DRUM (*Pogonias cromis*) ▮

▪ **RANGE:** Atlantic coast, from Delaware Bay to Florida; Gulf of Mexico.

▪ **WEIGHT:** Average 5–50 pounds, up to over 100 pounds.

Far less effective as a fighting fish is the black drum. Tough but relatively sluggish fighters, most are caught on bait, though they will take jigs and metal lures at times. Night fishing with clams on the bottom is the usual method in Delaware Bay, and the arrival of the fish is often announced by the drumming noise that can easily be heard above water.

Black drum are stockier than red drum, feature many barbels under the chin and have no dark spot on the tail base.

▮ WEAKFISH (*Cynoscion regalis*) ▮

▪ **RANGE:** Atlantic coast.

▪ **WEIGHT:** Average 2–10 pounds and up to 20 pounds.

Weakfish are pretty fish that resemble freshwater trout – leading to the common name of trout from Delaware south. In order to prevent confusion with the spotted sea trout from Chesapeake Bay south, weakfish are often referred to as gray trout. In New England, the Indian name, squeteague, is also common. Though not great fighters, weakfish are good sport on light tackle and a fine panfish. Gray trout found south of Cape Hatteras to Florida appear to be a separate population. While abundant in ocean areas just off the coasts of the Carolinas, they tend to be much smaller than in the north – and that's even more the case in Florida, especially with the scattering found on the Gulf side. The name weakfish refers to the easily-torn membrane of the mouth. Weakfish will hit a variety of baits and slow-moving lures.

▮ SPOTTED SEA TROUT (*Cynoscion nebulosus*) ▮

▪ **RANGE:** Atlantic coast from Florida to Virginia, and Gulf of Mexico.

▪ **WEIGHT:** Average 1–6 pounds, up to 20 pounds.

Though similar in shape to the weakfish, this species sports large black spots not only on its back and sides but also on the dorsal and caudal fins.

Spotted sea trout are similar to the weakfish in size, though larger specimens have become uncommon in recent years – possibly due to intense sport and commercial pressure on the species. Southern sportsmen are having some success in achieving game fish status for the species which, along with the redfish, accounts for a major portion of the inshore sport available along Gulf coasts.

▮ WHITE SEA BASS (*Atractoscion nobilis*) ▮

▪ **RANGE:** Pacific coast north to California.

▪ **WEIGHT:** Average 5–20 pounds, up to 100 pounds.

Southern California anglers seek this fish (a larger version of the weakfish and spotted sea trout) which frequents kelp beds off the coast. Unfortunately, fishing pressure has taken its toll on both the number and sizes of white sea bass caught in U.S. waters.

Tarpon
(Megalops atlantica)

■ **RANGE:** Atlantic coast from Florida to Virginia; Gulf of Mexico.
■ **WEIGHT:** Average 5–100 pounds, up to 300 pounds.

This large and rather primitive fish is most abundant in Florida, and the silver king is noted for its jumping ability.

Though they spawn at sea, tarpon are basically shallow-water fish – despite their size – being at home in rivers, creeks and even the Florida Keys flats. Fortunately, these fish are virtually inedible. Therefore, there's no commercial pressure on them, and the only threat to their survival is the disappearance of the mangrove swamps that are important in the life cycle of young tarpon.

Tarpon can be very fussy at times, but they'll usually fall for a live bait such as mullet or panfish. Live shrimp work well on the smaller tarpon found in creeks and under bridges at night. Lead-head jigs and virtually actionless lures such as the MirrOlure 52M are the usual choices for spinning and bait-casting gear, but fly casters do best of all on the flats since they can present the fly without spooking tarpon in shallow water. All tarpon should be released unless they are of record size.

Closely related to the tarpon is the **ladyfish** *(Elops saurus)*. Slender inshore game fish, averaging 2 to 4 pounds, they are superior fighters on light tackle and spend most of their time in the air. Ladyfish used to have the odd name "ten-pounder" – odd because it rarely, if ever, reached that weight. Ladyfish are primarily found in Florida, where they are particularly abundant in Florida Bay and the Ten Thousand Islands area of the southwest. They hit all sorts of small lures and, like the tarpon, aren't recommended for eating.

Bonefish
(Albula vulpes)

■ **RANGE:** Primarily Florida Keys.
■ **WEIGHT:** Average 3–8 pounds and up to 20 pounds.

The gray ghost of the flats is one of the prime angling attractions in the Florida Keys.

Traditional bonefishing is a combinating of hunting and fishing. Guides pole anglers along the flats and spy cruising bonefish with sunglasses – or observe them sticking their tails in the air while rooting out crabs, worms and shrimp from the bottom. The angler must then make an accurate cast which will enable him to put the bait (usually live shrimp) or lure (a tiny flatfish jig or a shrimp-like fly) in front of the fish – being sure not to spook the bonefish in the process. If the bonefish does hit, you'll be treated to a blistering run across the flats from a fish that won't quit until exhausted. It's also possible to catch bonefish without seeing them by seeding an area at the edge of a channel with pieces of shrimp and waiting for them to come to you. Bonefish are edible, but virtually all are returned to fight another day.

ABOVE *Author with a bonefish taken at dusk off Islamorada, Florida.*

OPPOSITE TOP *Weakfish are one of the most desired inshore fish along the Atlantic coast from North Carolina to Cape Cod. Francis Pandolfi, publisher of* Outdoor Life, Field & Stream *and* Salt Water Sportsman, *displays a large weakfish jigged off Block Island, Rhode Island.*

OPPOSITE BOTTOM *This distinctively marked spotted sea trout was caught on a lead-head jig in the Ten Thousand Islands out of Marco, Florida.*

ABOVE *Big barracuda such as this are common on Florida Keys flats. This one was caught near Key West and released.*

Snook
(Centropomus undecimalis)

■**RANGE:** Florida (both coasts); Texas.

■**WEIGHT:** Average 3–20 pounds, up to over 50 pounds.

This fine game fish is extremely sensitive to changes in water temperatures below 60 degrees Fahrenheit. Cold snaps in the winter often result in large snook kills when they're gathered in relatively shallow inland waters. These shallow-water fish work their way well up into rivers – often adapting to a freshwater environment. Snook are impossible to confuse with any other species, as they feature a black lateral line along silvery sides, the lower jaw protrudes, and the gill covers have sharp serrated edges that the angler must be aware of. Those gill covers are also line cutters and, as a result, snook fishermen often use Steelon or heavy mono leaders. Snook like to hang around mangrove roots, bridges and oyster bars to pounce on unwary bait fish passing by on the tide. They can be very fussy at times, but regularly fall for cast or trolled plugs and jigs. The best bet for a trophy snook is a live bait.

Barracuda

GREAT BARRACUDA (*Sphyraena barracuda*)

■ **RANGE:** Atlantic coast from Florida to North Carolina; Gulf of Mexico.

■ **WEIGHT:** Average 2–20 pounds.

Though about 20 species of barracuda occur throughout the world, this is the only one with blotches, which are distributed along the lower flanks. Barracuda are among the easiest fish to identify, and those nasty-looking teeth have led many to conclude that they are very dangerous to man. In actuality, barracuda are very curious and will stalk a diver – but will also back off immediately if the diver swims toward them. The only likelihood of becoming involved with the cuda's teeth (other than out of the water) would be in discolored water when the diver is wearing bright jewelry or dragging fish alongside his body. While the great barracuda poses no real threat in the water, this species is most frequently associated with ciguatera fish poisoning. Except in areas where there is no such problem, it's best not to consume this excellent-eating species – except for small specimens caught on the flats, rather than around reefs.

Since cuda can withstand lower water temperatures than bonefish and permit, guides often refer to them as "winter bonefish." These day-savers are at their best in the shallows as they hit tube lures skittered along the surface, and put on a beautiful aeriel display. Along the reef they hit lures and live baits, but don't endear themselves to sportsmen when they cut off other fish being fought to the boat.

BELOW *Captain Cal Cochran of Marathon, Florida, works the tube lure out of the mouth of a Content Keys barracuda before release.*

LEFT *Snook are one of the most popular inshore game fish in Florida waters, and also among the very best in the pan. Fortunately, they are a game fish in the Sunshine State.*

PACIFIC BARRACUDA (*Sphyraena argentea*)

■ **RANGE:** Pacific coast from southern California south.

■ **WEIGHT:** Up to 10 pounds.

Possible fish poisoning does not apply to the Pacific barracuda, a common species that is a popular party boat catch and a very good eating fish which carries no toxins.

C o b i a
(Rachycentron canadum)

■ **RANGE:** Florida and Gulf coasts, also off Virginia.
■ **WEIGHT:** Average below 70 pounds and up to 100 pounds.

This unusual-looking species is known as ling in the Gulf of Mexico. It somewhat resembles the remora or sharksucker, but lacks the sucking disc on the flattish head. The adults are generally chocolate-colored, and tend to gather around any obstruction or floating object, such as buoys, channel markers, bridges, oil rigs, wrecks and even boats. Uninformed anglers who spot cobia (which are great eaters) often think they are sharks and don't attempt to bait them.

Cobia strike readily at jigs and plugs, and they're the only fish other than barracuda which will regularly hit a tube lure skipped along the surface. However, it's hard to beat a live bait for cobia. Indeed, live baits are often used to lure cobia within casting range of fly-fishermen. Dead baits fished on bottom work in many areas. Cobia are not wary fish, and will sometimes come up from a wreck and hang around the boat waiting to be caught. They can be very good fighters, but always have plenty left when gaffed. As with the dolphin, the best best is to swing it right into the fish box and then sit on the lid.

S n a p p e r s

The Lutjanidae family includes many of the finest white-meated table fish in the world.

ABOVE *This big cobia was caught on a Gulf wreck off Key West.*

RIGHT *Mutton snappers are found on the flats as well as on reefs. This one was caught on a live crab while seeking permit in Biscayne Bay, Miami.*

■ RED SNAPPER (*Lutjanus campechanus*) ■
■ **RANGE:** Atlantic coast from Florida to North Carolina; Gulf of Mexico.
■ **WEIGHT:** Average 5–15 pounds and up to 50 pounds.

This bright red fish isn't great sport in the 40 fathom or greater depths it frequents, but they support a large party boat fishery from Gulf of Mexico ports.

About half the size of the red is the similar-looking **mutton snapper** (*Lutjanus analis*) of Florida waters. Though somewhat reddish, it has other colors on it including small blue streaks on the head, back and flanks plus orangish fins and a black, oval-shaped spot on the upper flank of each side. The mutton favors reef and inshore waters, even working onto the Keys flats. They are excellent fighters, and will strike jigs, live and dead baits, and even flies.

CUBERA (*Lutjanus cyanopterus*)

■ **RANGE:** Southern Florida.

■ **WEIGHT:** Up to over 120 pounds.

Largest of the American snappers though an unimpressive grayish color, the cubera flashes some very imposing teeth. It is a relatively rare species (most common off Florida), which is caught primarily while fishing the reef at night. Those seeking it specifically often sacrifice a spiny lobster for bait.

GRAY SNAPPER (*Lutjanus griseus*)

■ **RANGE:** Florida (both coasts).

■ **WEIGHT:** Average 1–5 pounds and up to 15–20 pounds.

Though it's also common on the inner reef, the gray (also known as mangrove) is most often associated with mangrove creeks and rivers. Though not as colorful as most other snappers, it's a fine fighting fish that readily hits live and dead baits as well as jigs and plugs. Fishing for them is usually best at night. Walk around just about any dock in the Keys and you'll be able to see gray snappers. They'll eat anything thrown to them, as long as there's no line attached. Rarely will the wary gray make a mistake. If one does, that will serve to warn the rest of the school to be even more wary.

YELLOWTAIL SNAPPER (*Ocyurus chrysurus*)

■ **RANGE:** Florida Keys.

■ **WEIGHT:** Average 1–3 pounds, up to 10 pounds.

This beautiful and delicious snapper frequents the Florida Keys reefs, where many rod-and-reel fishermen make a living catching them for market by chumming with glass minnows and other small bait fish plus ground chum. They are fine fighters on light tackle, and although normally quite wary, yellowtails are known to go wild when live pilchards are spread over the reef. This colorful species has a yellow stripe that extends all along the body.

TOP Former baseball great Boog Powell with a yellowtail snapper caught off Key West.

ABOVE Gray (mangrove) snappers are abundant around docks and bridges in southeast Florida, but are hard to catch except at night. This one was caught off a Florida Keys bridge.

VERMILLION SNAPPER (*Rhomboplites aurorubens*)

■ **RANGE:** Florida Keys.

■ **WEIGHT:** 1–4 pounds.

This is a small, slim reddish species which is common on the offshore snapper banks.

Sea bass

The sea bass family Serranideae also includes many similar looking species of grouper, which are warm water bottom fish. Grouper identifications are difficult, as all are capable of color change – making that an unreliable guide from area to area. It's probably that very factor which has prevented the IGFA from maintaining line class records on all but the jewfish. Nevertheless, most groupers are good fighters as bottom fish go. They're also outstanding food fish, though some have been implicated in ciguatera poisoning. The yellowfin grouper in the Bahamas has a particularly bad reputation in that regard.

The striped bass (featured earlier in this section) is not part of the Serranideae family, but rather a member of the temperate bass family Percichthyidae. A grouper look-alike, the **giant sea bass** (*Stereolepis gigas*) of the Pacific is also a member of the Percichthyidae family. This long-lived fish grows to over 600 pounds and is caught from southern California to Mexico. Several of the largest specimens were boated off Catalina Island, California. Live and dead baits fished on heavy tackle in 10 to 25 fathoms over rocky bottoms and around kelp beds will lure this huge fish.

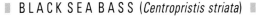

BLACK SEA BASS (*Centropristis striata*)

■ RANGE: Atlantic coast from Florida to Massachusetts, also Gulf of Mexico.
■ WEIGHT: Average 1–2 pounds and up to 10 pounds.

Among the sea bass of the Serranidae family this species is of greatest interest to anglers. They put up a good scrap when hooked on dead baits (usually squid or clams) off bottom. Black sea bass are hermaphrodites (they begin life as females and change to males as they grow larger). The big ones develop a bluish hump just behind their heads and are referred to as humpbacks. Many of the groupers have a similar life cycle.

Though the catch varies from year-to-year, black sea bass normally are one of the top few species in terms of both numbers and weight caught by anglers in the mid-Atlantic and are also highly esteemed as food fish – particularly in Chinese restaurants.

KELP BASS (*Paralabrax clathratus*)

■ RANGE: Pacific coast from central California south.
■ SIZE: Up to 1½ feet.

An important West Coast sea bass, the kelp bass is a small species growing to about 1½ feet. It is found from central California south, and is one of the most abundant species taken by party boat anglers fishing around kelp beds.

Californians also catch lots of **barred sand bass** (*Paralabrax nebulifer*), which grow to about 12 pounds, on rocky and sandy bottoms, as well as the similar **spotted sand bass** (*Paralabrax maculatofasciatus*), which has black spots.

OPPOSITE *The author hoists a 50-pound jewfish caught on a Gulf of Mexico wreck, in 60 feet, off the Florida Keys.*

TOP *Kelp bass are a popular target for California anglers.*

ABOVE *Black sea bass do not come much bigger than this one caught off Montauk, New York.*

JEWFISH (Epinephelus itajara)

■ RANGE: Florida (both coasts).

■ WEIGHT: Up to 800 pounds.

Among the groupers, the jewfish is the largest and the Atlantic counterpart of the giant sea bass. This shallow water species is most abundant around wrecks in the Gulf of Mexico but also tends to lay in holes under bridges and docks, in channels and even on the Florida Keys flats. The body of this large-mouthed grouper is covered with spots and blotches.

Jewfish are hooked on both live and dead baits, and must be muscled away from wherever they live or the angler will be cut off in short order. Smaller jewfish are more active and will even strike at jigs.

WARSAW GROUPER (Epinephelus nigritus)

■ RANGE: Florida; Gulf of Mexico

■ WEIGHT: Average under 100 pounds and up to 500 pounds.

A step below the jewfish, this species is found more frequently around deeper wrecks on the east coast of Florida. The Warsaw's body is uniformly dark, with no spots.

BLACK GROUPER (Mycteroperca bonaci)

■ RANGE: Florida.

■ WEIGHT: Up to 100 pounds.

Among the commonly-caught groupers this species is the largest. It can be identified by the dark body color combined with a broad, dark outer zone on the soft dorsal, anal and caudal fins set off by a white margin. The black is one of the most aggressive groupers, and will readily hit baits and lures trolled over the reef.

YELLOWFIN GROUPER (Mycteroperca venenosa)

■ RANGE: Southern Florida.

■ WEIGHT: Up to 30 pounds and more.

This species has dark brown blotches arranged in lengthwise rows plus numerous small, dark reddish spots. The outer edges of the pectoral fins are sharply defined with a broad orange zone.

GAG GROUPER (Mycteroperca microlepis)

■ RANGE: Atlantic coast to North Carolina; Gulf of Mexico.

■ WEIGHT: Average 5 pounds and up to 60 pounds.

The gag is often confused with the black grouper, which is a larger species. It can be separated from the black by its pale body, indistinct dark blotches and the whitish edges of the caudal, dorsal and anal fins plus the first ray of the ventral fins.

SCAMP (Mycteroperca phenax)

■ RANGE: South Atlantic, Gulf of Mexico.

■ WEIGHT: Up to 10 pounds.

This is a small grouper with numerous small brown spots on body and fins; it may well be the best-eating member of the family.

ABOVE *Red groupers are the most common of the family.*

LEFT *Big black groupers, like these 40-pounders, are taken at night in the Tortugas west of Key West.*

▌ RED GROUPER (*Epinephelus morio*) ▌

■ **RANGE:** South Atlantic and Gulf of Mexico.
■ **WEIGHT:** Up to 30 pounds and more.

One of the more common members of the family, they can be identified (in addition to the red coloration – which is highly variable) by the green eyes and the elevation of the second dorsal spine.

Cod

ABOVE *A yellowfin grouper.*

The cod family Gadidae includes some of the most important food fish in the world, and many are also of great interest to anglers. All of these fish live in cold waters, primarily in the Atlantic. In some cases, almost identical species live in the North Pacific and are of great commercial importance – but not readily accessible to sportsmen.

▌ COD (*Gadus morhua*) ▌

■ **RANGE:** North Atlantic, especially from New Jersey to Maine and Maritime Provinces.
■ **WEIGHT:** Average 3–30 pounds, with maximum of 100 pounds. 210 pounds recorded in 19th century.

The giant of this family, and the species which tempted European fishermen across the Atlantic to the banks off Newfoundland hundreds of years ago. Still one of the most prolific and important ground fish, the cod is subject to intense pressures. It was severely depleted by foreign fleets in the 1960s, and has more recently taken a beating from a domestic commercial fleet which has built up tremendously since the

RIGHT *The author with a big pollock caught from a deepwater wreck in New York Bight.*

cod population rebounded after the 200-mile limit was enacted. Ever-stricter regulations by the New England Fisheries Management Council are required in order to prevent over-exploitation.

Cod are primarily caught by bottom fishing on offshore grounds and wrecks, though they also move very close to shore from Cape Cod north. Bait fishing (clams, herring, squid, etc.) is the usual method, but many are also caught on diamond jigs.

The very similar **Pacific cod** (*Gadus macrocephalus*) is a smaller fish found from Oregon north but is of no great angling importance.

▌ HADDOCK (*Melanogrammus aeglefinus*) ▌

■ **RANGE:** North Atlantic, mainly north of Cape Cod.
■ **WEIGHT:** Average 3–6 pounds and up to 20 pounds.

Of almost equal commercial importance as the cod, the haddock suffers even more from commercial fishing. It is easily distinguished by the plain gray sides with a distinct black lateral line and a large dark blotch over the pectoral fin. Haddock are sought after by New England fishermen working offshore grounds on party boats. Most are caught on baits fished over more open bottom than that frequented by cod.

▌ POLLOCK (*Pollachius virens*) ▌

■ **RANGE:** North Atlantic.
■ **WEIGHT:** Average 5–30 pounds and up to 50 pounds.

This species covers more of the water column than the cod and haddock. It's an active predator which is regularly jigged at mid-depths as it pursues schools of squid, herring and sand eels. Pollock tend to lay over wrecks, and that is where most are caught, though they are the best fighting member of the cod family.

Pollock are not as desirable for eating as cod and haddock, but there's still a large commercial fishery for them.

The smaller **walleye pollock** (*Theragra chalcogramma*) of the North Pacific is taken commercially in huge quantities, and is the inexpensive white meat fillet usually utilized in fast food fish sandwiches.

The closely-related hakes include a few species of interest to anglers. The **white hake** (*Urophycis tenuis*) is a large, sluggish fish which grows to over 60 pounds and frequents wrecks and rough bottoms from New Jersey north. The similar-looking **red hake** (*Urophycis chuss*) is much smaller (up to about 8 pounds) but also far more abundant. Known locally as ling in the Metropolitan New York area, it's an important food fish that attracts many anglers to party boats from fall through spring. Though red hake gather primarily around wrecks and on rough bottoms from 2 to 20 miles offshore, they also move right into the beach at times from November to January and again from March to April. Both white and red hake have tasty but soft flesh that must be kept cool.

However, the **silver hake** (*Merluccius bilinearis*) is a quite different-looking slim, silvery species with firmer meat. It's also a small fish (averaging less than one pound), but very popular in the Metropolitan New York area. Their movements are similar to those of the red hake, though they live on more open bottoms and actually chase bait fish

TOP *Michael Ristori with one of the small cod that keep anglers busy through the winter on wrecks in New York Bight.*

ABOVE *The Atlantic cod is one of the most important food and sport fish in the Northeast.*

into the wash during early winter. At such times they may strand themselves on the beaches and be almost instantly frozen – leading to the name frostfish. However, this very popular winter party boat species is best-known as whiting around the Metropolitan area. Both red and silver hake are more abundant in New England offshore waters, but there's virtually no angling interest in them there.

Flounder

The order Pleuronectiformes is divided into the lefteye flounders Bothidae and the righteye flounders Pleuronectidae. All flounders start life as ordinary looking fish, but they quickly flatten out and one eye migrates to the top side of the body. Their flatness permits the flounder to lay on the bottom or even to dig in – ready to pounce on anything edible passing by. There are many species and all are excellent eating fish.

SUMMER FLOUNDER (*Paralichthys dentatus*)

■ **RANGE:** Mid-Atlantic.

■ **WEIGHT:** Average 1–2 pounds and up to 25 pounds.

The lefteye group is led by the summer flounder, one of the top few angling species in the Mid-Atlantic. Summer flounder are known as fluke from New Jersey to Cape Cod, and simply as flounder south to the Carolinas. The party boat fishery of the Mid-Atlantic is basically dependent on this species and the bluefish, but fluke are also under tremendous commercial pressure – and regulations have been placed on both fisheries in order to prevent a serious decline.

Fluke are inshore fish which spread into bays and rivers, and respond to many dead and live baits fished on bottom. They're more aggressive than most flounders, and movement of the bait is essential. Therefore drifting is the normal fishing method.

The similar **southern flounder** (*Paralichthys lethostigma*) replaces the summer flounder below the Carolinas and into the Gulf of Mexico. Achieving similar sizes, larger specimens are more uncommon.

ABOVE *The silver hake is known as whiting in the Metropolitan New York area, where it is a very important winter and spring species.*

ABOVE RIGHT *A trio of "doormat" fluke caught off Montauk Point, New York.*

CALIFORNIA HALIBUT (*Paralichthys californicus*)

RANGE: Pacific coast from Baja California to San Francisco.
WEIGHT: Averaging 5–20 pounds, up to 75 pounds.
other important lefteye flounder, this highly sought-after flatfish is an important and highly sought-after party boat catch of the California coast. They frequent waters of 10 to 20 fathoms over sandy bottoms, and are usually caught by drifting with baits on the bottom.

ATLANTIC HALIBUT (*Hippoglossus hippoglossus*)

RANGE: North Atlantic.
WEIGHT: Averaging 50–100 pounds, up to 700 pounds.
The righteye flounders include the two giants of the family. This is the largest of all, but it was long ago fished out by commercial fishermen to such an extent that it's no more than an incidental catch now even in prime areas and an Atlantic halibut of any size is a prize catch.

▌ PACIFIC HALIBUT (*Hippoglossus stenolepis*) ▌

■ **RANGE:** North Pacific, especially Alaska.
■ **WEIGHT:** Average 30–150 pounds and up to 500 pounds.

An intensive commercial fishery conducted by both the U.S. and Canada has long been strictly regulated by international agreement, which is probably why there's still a very good summer sport fishery in Alaska close to shore. As is the case with the Atlantic halibut, they are taken on both baits and diamond jigs fished on bottom but are a far easier target for the angler.

▌ WINTER FLOUNDER (*Pseudopleuronectes americanus*) ▌

■ **RANGE:** Atlantic, New Jersey to Canadian Maritime Provinces.
■ **WEIGHT:** Average ½–1½ pounds, up to 8 pounds.

In terms of volume this is the most important righteyed flounder to anglers. This species is abundant in the spring and fall in Mid-Atlantic and southern New England bays and rivers.

The species (called blackback in New England) summers offshore, but returns to the shallows as the waters cool – spending the winter bedded down in the bottom before spawning when water temperatures rise. In northern New England and the Maritime Provinces they can be found in shallow waters all summer. Winter flounder have very small mouths and are caught on slim, soft baits such as seaworms, mussels and strips of clam.

Pacific anglers concentrate on the **starry flounder** (*Platichthys stellatus*), which can reach 20 pounds and features patches of shiny star-like scales on its body, and the **diamond turbot** (*Hypsopetta guttulata*), a diamond-shaped flatfish running up to 4 pounds.

Other important species

ABOVE One of the largest members of the cod family, Pacific halibut provide a good summer sport fishery in the Pacific.

RIGHT The hogfish bears little resemblance to the other wrasses, but this reef and wreck inhabitant of southern Florida waters is highly prized as a food fish.

The wrasse family Labridae consists primarily of small, colorful tropical species, but the most important member is a blackish species favoring cool waters. The **tautog** (*Tautoga onitis*) is recognized by the IGFA as a game fish, and provides lots of bottom fishing action from Virginia north to Cape Cod. In addition, some isolated pockets of tautog may be found in Pamlico Sound, North Carolina, and

LEFT Author with a winter flounder, a very important inshore bottom fish from New Jersey to Maine.

ABOVE *A sheepshead from Marco, Florida.*

Charleston Harbor, South Carolina. The common name in New York and New Jersey is blackfish, but tautog is used both north and south of there. They are basically a spring and fall species in inshore waters, though some remain active in 100-foot depths in New York Bight during the winter. Tautog are crab eaters with specialized protruding front teeth and crushers in the mouth. As a result, they can be quite difficult to hook on the green or fiddler crab baits generally used. Most range from 1 to 5 pounds, but 10-pounders aren't uncommon – and the maximum size is well over 20 pounds.

Also of angling interest in the wrasse family is the colorful **California sheepshead** (*Semicossyphus pulcher*) which is found from Monterey Bay south and can grow to well over 30 pounds. The **hogfish** (*Lachnolaimus maximus*) is another colorful member of the family. It is found on reefs off southeast Florida, and runs up to 20 pounds.

The porgy family Sparidae is headed by the **scup** (called porgy south of New England) which is a small but very abundant fish. This broadsided, silvery battler is a tough customer on light tackle. Vast numbers are caught from Long Island east to Martha's Vineyard, with a large fleet of boats fishing them from June to October off Montauk, Long Island. Small scup are taken in good numbers off the New Jersey coast in the fall, but, there isn't much fishing for them south of the Garden State. Young scup move into inland waters and are called bay porgies, while the adults favor rough bottom areas not too far offshore. A scup of 3 pounds is considered very large, but they do run up to 6 pounds.

Some larger, similar-looking porgies are caught in offshore waters from the Carolinas to Florida, but the most important warm-water member is the **sheepshead** (*Archosargus probatocephalus*), which has a porgy-like body with prominent black stripes, but teeth like a tautog. It can weigh as much as 25 pounds, and is usually caught with crabs or shrimp around docks, bridges, wrecks and other obstructions from North Carolina to Texas.

The sculpin family Cottidae is not a popular one in the Atlantic, due to the horny heads and sharp spines present in most species. However, the **cabezon** (*Scorpaenichthys marmoratus*) of the Pacific coast weighs up to 25 pounds and is a prize catch for bottom fishermen.

The scorpion fish family Scorpaenidae includes some of the most poisonous stingers in the world (especially the stonefish and zebrafish of the Indo-Pacific), but the various rockfish in that family are angling favorites on the Pacific coast. Most important of the many species are the **bocaccio** (*Sebastes paucispinis*) which can grow to 20 pounds, the **chilipepper** (*Sebastes goodei*), and the **blue rockfish** (*Sebastes mystinus*) which frequents shallow waters.

The greenling family Hexagrammidae consists primarily of small Pacific species, but includes one very important game fish – the mis-named **lingcod** (*Ophiodon elongatus*), which grows to at least 70 pounds and is common in cool waters from near-shore areas out to great depths. This fine-eating species is pursued by both sport and commercial fishermen. Anglers catch them with bait or jigs fished on bottom.

Chapter Four
TECHNIQUE & STRATEGY

The modern angler has all the tools at his fingertips, both in terms of equipment and knowledge. As a result, even though the quantities of fish may not be what they were in previous generations, we can search out concentrations that weren't even suspected in the "good old days."

The learning process

Among the sources of information available are newspapers, radio, TV, magazines, books and videos. Good newspapers in saltwater areas not only provide up-to-date information about fishing conditions on Fridays, but also include party and charter boat advertising. This is the most current information you can obtain from a public source unless there's a radio or TV show in your area. Weekly fishing magazines have sprung up in many areas, and they're particularly good at providing "how-to-fish" data about local hot spots. Only a few monthly magazines on the national level contain enough saltwater material to make them worthwhile. Entirely saltwater are the *Salt Water Sportsman* and the newer *Sport Fishing*, while *Fishing World* is about 50 percent saltwater. For gaining a great deal of information on a particular subject, it's hard to beat books written by knowledgeable authors. Videos are becoming an ever more important teaching tool, as they permit you to visualize what is being explained.

In terms of learning how to fish for a species or how to work an area, there's nothing better than joining an experienced angler. You can join a fishing club with similar interests to your own, and by inquiring around you'll be able to determine which clubs are oriented toward inshore boat fishing, offshore fishing, surfcasting, saltwater fly-fishing, etc. Once in the club you'll have the opportunity to meet experienced anglers and possibly get invited on some trips.

Another good source of information is the tackle shop and marina. Keep your ears open and don't hesitate to ask questions. It may pay in the long run to spend more for your equipment at a local tackle shop with an ear to the fishing than saving a few dollars at a discount store.

Even if you own a boat, it's often a good idea to charter an experienced captain once before attempting a new type of fishing yourself. You'll probably do much better than you would have on your own, and the experience provided should more than pay for itself as you pursue that aspect of the sport in the future.

Make sure your boat is properly equipped with Loran C, fishfinder, water temperature gauge and VHF radio at the very minimum. Then obtain fishing charts for the areas you'll be working. Such charts are available in tackle shops or by mail, and should provide Loran C numbers for all popular fishing areas and wrecks plus courses and distances from various area inlets. Those charts are worth their weight in gold to both novice and expert. In combination with your electronics, you can be fishing in the right places even without experience. Of course, knowing how to catch fish once you're there is another matter altogether.

OPPOSITE *The author was surprised by this 32-pound striped bass which hit a small tube rigged on the leader above a diamond jig – he was using a very slow retrieve just off bottom for weakfish.*

TOP *An angler fights a shark aboard as a fellow angler stands by with the tagging stick.*

ABOVE *This angler learned his lesson about dressing warmly for winter fishing and is fully equipped to catch silver hake (whiting) in February off the New Jersey coast.*

BELOW *Heavy clothing is required in cold weather areas enabling the angler to be on the water when the fish are biting. The author hoists a 58-pound striped bass taken while trolling at night on Shagwong Reef off Montauk, New York.*

Fishing strategies

Fishing should be approached just as any other competition is. Develop a game plan for each trip, but be prepared to make changes as circumstances dictate. Determine all the possibilities beforehand, and take along whatever might be required. I hate to drag along so much gear on each trip, but would rather do that than get into a surprising flurry of action with an untargeted species and not have anything along to catch them with. The same thing applies in terms of clothing for cold weather fishing. No matter how nice the weather forecast, always dress for the worst.

By using all the sources of information described in *Saltwater Fishing Skills*, and developing the "feel" described in that chapter, you'll be able to significantly improve the number of good days. Conditions change so rapidly in saltwater fishing that the presence of fish in a given spot one day is no assurance that they'll be there the next. Chances are good that the fish will stay put if conditions remain the same, but a shift in wind direction or speed can change everything.

Remember to keep all the variables in mind, even though experience will enable you to isolate periods of prime fishing, it's always worthwhile to keep a line in the water.

Every type of fishing requires different strategies, and it's important that you not get hooked on only reacting in certain ways. The proper way to hook one bottom fish may be a sure recipe for failure with another that hits differently. Bluefish, striped bass and weakfish often feed in the same areas, but the usual fast retrieve of a diamond jig will usually produce only the currently less desirable bluefish. However, by working the jig very slowly off bottom it's possible to tempt some stripers and weakfish from among the voracious choppers. It's little tricks like that which often separate the professionals from other fishermen. Get to know the species you're seeking, and you'll soon figure out the little tricks which may make all the difference.

Netting & gaffing

Gaffs are rarely used in freshwater situations, but are standard in the briny when fish aren't to be released. Select gaffs appropriate for your fishing, and always have a spare on board. Strong fish like the tunas should be gaffed in the head or just behind it. In this fashion they can be easily controlled by pulling the head out of the water. However, a tail-gaffed tuna can be a real problem. Regardless of what type of gaff you're using, be sure to take your time to get a good shot. In most cases it's much better to let the fish make another run rather than taking a desperate stab at it. Place yourself aft of the angler (so you don't have to work around the line) and have him bring the fish to you. Lay the gaff over the fish's back and pull back with authority. Sharks are best handled with flying gaffs (see *Saltwater Fishing Tackle*) due to their habit of spinning when restrained, which can result in a straight gaff being pulled out of your hands.

Nets are fine for many smaller species that make a small target for gaffing or which are to be released. Avoid using nets on sharp-toothed species, such as bluefish, or where plugs are being used. Getting a bunch of trebles hung up in a net can result in your spending most of the day removing them instead of fishing. Be sure the net you're using is wide enough to accommodate the species sought. Small summer flounder (fluke) will fit nicely into ordinary nets, but a very large model is needed for a doormat. Never try to net fish tail first. They can escape easily as soon as they feel themselves being trapped. A big problem with nets when you're using them properly (head-on) is that the fish can see the net and may panic if not exhausted.

It's not always necessary to gaff or net fish. Especially from small boats, most fish can be lifted over when heavy leaders are used, and this will avoid all the blood from gaffing or the hassle of getting fish and hooks out of nets. Even when a leader isn't used, it may be possible to grab a diamond jig or jig head sticking out of the fish's mouth and swing it aboard. Don't try this with treble-hooked plugs!

BELOW *Anglers on West Coast long range boats bring lots of gear with them. This is only a portion of one fisherman's tackle on the Royal Polaris from San Diego, California.*

LEFT *The author places the gaff in this large Key West barracuda's mouth so the tube lure could be removed and the fish released without much handling.*

RIGHT Bill Munro of Mako Marine demonstrates another means of handling barracuda for release.

Handling the catch

There's a great variation among saltwater species in how much care must be taken to keep them in prime eating condition. As a general rule, try to get anything you catch on ice as soon as possible – preferably after being cleaned. That's especially important with fish like the bluefish which have strong stomach acids. On the other hand, fish such as the striped bass are sent to market whole. Some species require special attention. Tuna should be bled immediately upon gaffing, and most sharks must be bled and gutted as soon as they can be safely handled. Fish flesh is best when absolutely fresh, and deteriorates steadily thereafter. Carefully wrap and quick-freeze any fish not being utilized within a couple of days – and then consume it within three months.

Though build-ups of certain toxics have been found in various species living near heavily populated or industrial areas, there is little to fear from eating fish in general. Even where toxics are present, almost all can be eliminated by filleting and skinning the fish – thus doing away with the internal organs and belly flap. To complete the job, strip out all the dark meat along the middle of the fillet – as that oily portion concentrates any contaminants. Broiling will further remove any oils that may remain. Of course, all shellfish from even slightly contaminated areas should be avoided – as should fish that don't migrate from such areas. Check with your state's health agency for local guidance.

Release fishing

While the concept of releasing fish to fight another day has long been popular in freshwater recreational fishing, it's only recently caught on to any great extent in marine areas. This is primarily due to the fact that anglers often feel they're releasing fish only for them to be caught by netters. However, more restrictions are being placed on

LEFT A tagged yellowfin tuna.

ABOVE With a heavy enough leader, it is often easier to just swing small fish, such as this dolphin, aboard.

ABOVE *This striped bass,
caught off Island Beach
State Park, New Jersey,
sports a U.S. Fish &
Wildlife Service tag.*

ABOVE RIGHT *A tag has been
placed in this small blue
marlin caught off Key West.*

commercial fishing all the time – and sportsmen have responded to the severe declines in such species as striped bass, red drum, snook and king mackerel by more frequently releasing even those specimens larger than the new minimums. Hopefully, this developing sporting ethic will continue and flourish as fish populations are restored by strict management measures.

If you are going to release fish, do so very carefully. Try to prevent bleeding, and handle the fish so as not to harm it. In the case of fish without sharp teeth, such as the striped bass, it's possible to obtain a firm grasp on the jaw. Toothy critters may have to be gripped by the gill cover, but be sure you place your hand between the gill cover and gills – and not into the gill rakers themselves. In any case, do as little handling as possible (cut off deeply-hooked fish, rather than attempt to remove the hook) and avoid removing the protective slime coating from the fish.

As long as you're releasing fish, why not tag them. One tagging program available to all is that sponsored by the American Littoral Society, Sandy Hook, Highlands, NJ 07732. Members ($20 per year) buy tagging kits which can be used on any species worldwide. If returned, the angler receives information about where and when the fish was caught and how large it became – plus a patch. Many fishing clubs have set up similar programs for specific species.

In a few cases, government gets involved in working with sportsmen to increase the number of certain tagged fish. For instance, the National Marine Fisheries Service Cooperative Shark Tagging Program (Narragansett Laboratory, South Ferry Rd., Narragansett, RI 02882) is basically dependent on volunteer tagging by sport fishermen. The same applies to NMFS Cooperative Gamefish Tagging Programs which are run on both coasts. The Atlantic program (NMFS Miami Laboratory, 75 Virginia Beach Dr., Miami, FL 33149) is concerned with tunas, billfish and king mackerel. The Pacific study (NMFS La Jolla Laboratory, P.O. Box 271, La Jolla, CA 92038) is for billfish only, though the same lab also runs a tagging program for albacore. The government programs provide tags to sportsmen at no charge for the species indicated. Some states have set up similar tagging programs for inshore species.

Taking care of tackle

A nice day at sea can be ruined by tackle that malfunctions and, more often than not, the fault is with the angler rather than the manufacturer. It's easy enough to care for tackle if a little time is devoted to it at the end of each trip. Most reels are now made with materials that won't rust away at the first sight of saltwater, but the briny is still tough on gear that would stand up for years in sweetwater fishing. At the very minimum, sprinkle your tackle with fresh water. Even better, liberally apply WD-40 or similar formulations to all your rods and reels. It won't hurt anything, including your line, and will lock out that destructive salt. After a season of hard use, the return of reels to the factory or a local repair station over the winter will assure you of a good start for the following season. Rusting of hooks is another frequent problem, and many saltwater anglers avoid this by carrying a bucket of fresh water on the boat and dropping every used plug in that bucket as soon as they're finished fishing it.

LEFT *A blue shark is fought off Montauk, as the mate stands by with a tagging stick.*

Chapter Five

WHERE TO GO

This is strictly a book-length subject on its own! However, as a general introduction there follows a brief overview of what the saltwater angler can expect to encounter along the coasts of Canada and the United States at various times of the year.

Maritime provinces

Saltwater sport fishing is basically a summer sport. There are lots of cod, pollock, winter flounder and mackerel in this area close to, or right from, shore.

Giant bluefin tuna are the only big game species, but the largest specimens in the world have been caught in waters around Prince Edward Island, New Brunswick and Nova Scotia. The greatest of them all (at this writing) was the 1496-pound giant caught by Ken Fraser at the Canso Causeway area of Nova Scotia on October 26, 1979. In that area, any tuna caught during the late-October to early-November run is considered small if under 1000 pounds. However, giant tuna runs have been getting poorer there, as well as at nearby North Lake, Prince Edward Island – where the prime period is from September through mid-October. Giant tuna have favored different areas of Canada over the decades. Wedgeport, Nova Scotia, was originally the hot spot, but they disappeared there. Then there were huge schools of giants at Newfoundland in the 1960s, but they too moved on. Prince Edward Island later produced the first 1000-pounder, and North Lake became famed as a tuna port.

Giant tuna fishing is restricted to commercial fishermen in Canada, but some of them take out anglers for relatively low fees. Striped bass may be caught in Nova Scotia, where they appear to be a holdover population – rather than migratory.

Northern New England

The fisheries from Cape Cod north are quite different from those of the cape to the south. Featured are such cold-water species as cod, haddock, pollock, mackerel and the very occasional halibut. These species are pursued by many party boats operating out of Massachusetts, New Hampshire and Maine ports. As a general rule, very large diamond jigs are used for cod and pollock on the offshore banks of the Gulf of Maine – while haddock are caught on bait. Giant bluefin tuna are a popular target on Stellwagen Bank, with Gloucester, Green Harbor and Provincetown, Massachusetts, being the primary ports. That fishing is primarily chunking, but many giants are trolled in Cape Cod Bay in early summer and early fall. Winter flounder and harbor pollock are abundant for shore anglers, and tautog are at the northern end of their range in Cape Cod Bay. Striped bass fishing is the prime sport for inshore anglers throughout the region, and bluefish are abundant right up to Maine during the peaks of their cycles – but may disappear for many years thereafter.

OPPOSITE Rental boat anglers set off for a day's fishing in Peconic Bay.

ABOVE In 1972, before giant tuna were worth the money to ship them, they were stacked up like cordwood at Provincetown, Massachusetts, after a tournament on Stellwagen Bank in Massachusetts Bay.

ABOVE *Happy party boat anglers with cod, pollock and white hake after a trip off southern New England.*

Southern New England

Though the northern species are still found south of Cape Cod, this area also plays host to warmer water species from spring through fall. Striped bass fishing is very important, and such areas as Pleasant Bay, the Outer Cape, Nantucket, Martha's Vineyard, Cuttyhunk, Narragansett and Block Island have long been famous. Cod fishing is good even during the summer on Cox's Ledge and offshore wrecks, and winter flounder fishing is outstanding in the spring from Connecticut to Cape Cod. Summer flounder (fluke) also provide good action in warmer weather, and there is outstanding porgy and sea bass fishing. Tautog are at their best in southern New England, with prime fishing during the spring and fall. Offshore fishermen can enjoy the full range of northern sport from giant bluefins close to shore out to moderate range sharks and school tuna and finally to tropical variety in the canyons. Bluefish are thick throughout the area, and some of the largest are caught at the western end of Long Island Sound as they hound schools of bunkers. Point Judith, Rhode Island hosts one of the largest charter and party boat fleets in the country.

New York & New Jersey

These states boast many great sport fishing ports. Montauk, at the east end of Long Island, may have the best all-round fishing in the world during the summer and early fall. Sheepshead Bay, in Brooklyn, probably has the largest party boat fleet in the world – including many over 100 feet in length. Other major New York ports include Greenport, Shinnecock, Captree, Freeport and Point Lookout. New Jersey has large party and charter boat fleets at Atlantic Highlands, Highlands, Belmar, Brielle, Point Pleasant, Barnegat Light, Wildwood, Cape May and Fortescue. Local fishing is similar to that of southern New England, but many more boats in New York Bight regularly make the long runs to the canyons and other offshore fishing areas. Shark fishing is very important in June, when makos move within 20 to 40 miles of the coasts. Bluefish are caught in the greatest quantities in New York Bight, and are the favored party boat fish along with summer flounder (fluke.) Fishing continues right through winter for cod, red hake (ling,) silver hake (whiting) and tautog (blackfish.) All-in-all, New York Bight has some of the best fishing in the world despite the population of the region.

Mid-Atlantic

Fishing gradually changes from Delaware to Cape Hatteras. Some warm-water species are common only as far as Delaware Bay (such as black drum,) and such cool-water inhabitants as cod, pollock, winter flounder and giant tuna are almost absent. Chesapeake Bay is famed as the principal spawning area for the striped bass. Weakfishing is best there and in Delaware Bay. Ocean City, Maryland, is noted as a white marlin port, while Virginia Beach, Virginia, is the northernmost port producing substantial numbers of blue marlin. Oregon Inlet and Hatteras, North Carolina, are relatively close to the Gulf Stream, and provide the best northern opportunity for blue and white marlin, dolphin and wahoo. Pamlico Sound, North Carolina, has a good cobia fishery, and red drum (channel bass) are the featured species on the Outer Banks of North Carolina.

South Atlantic

The area from south of Cape Hatteras to Georgia is best-known for inshore sport with spotted sea trout and smaller red drum (puppy drum.) Cobia are a prime summer species, and even tarpon reach these waters in some quantity. Amberjack are abundant on offshore wrecks, and party boats sail far offshore to seek out red snappers and groupers. Big game anglers must make long runs over a shallow continental shelf in order to reach blue water.

TOP *Blue marlin being weighed in during a tournament at Hatteras, North Carolina.*

ABOVE *Surfcasters working on striped bass at Montauk Point, New York, in the fall.*

Florida

No other state has such variety. During the winter, the best fishing occurs in southeast Florida from Cape Canaveral to the Keys. Sail fishing is best from Fort Pierce to Palm Beach in mid-winter, and migratory amberjack and cobia are at their peak on Keys wrecks at the same time. However, spring is a much better time to seek bonefish and permit on Keys flats. Tarpon fishing opens up in Key West Harbor in February, and that area may have the most consistent and convenient fishing for large tarpon in the world. Indeed, Key West is one of the great sport fishing ports in the world – with outstanding reef, flats, offshore and wreck fishing. The tarpon run gradually extends up both coasts in the spring. Northeastern Florida gets all of the southern sport during the summer, except bonefish, permit and some reef species. The Gulf Coast gets a better shot at blue marlin in the summer, though that fishing is well offshore of such ports as Destin. The Panhandle also boasts fine cobia fishing in the spring, while Homosassa is famed for its giant tarpon at the same time – and Boca Grande Pass is called the "tarpon capital of the world." The Marco area in southwest Florida offers access to the still-wild Ten Thousand Islands and great light-tackle fishing for spotted sea trout, red drum, snook, tarpon, ladyfish and many other species.

Gulf Coast

Inshore fishing in Alabama, Mississippi, Louisiana and Texas features spotted sea trout and red drum. Conservation efforts have insured that these fisheries will not be fished out in the near future. Oil rigs provide outstanding sport fishing for a great variety of fish, many of which were rarely caught in this area before the rigs were put in. Even pompano frequent the rigs, though their numbers have been depleted by commercial fishing. Cobia, amberjack, groupers, snappers and many other species are taken at the rigs – with the cast of species changing as water depth does. King mackerel (kingfish) used to be the major offshore species, but that fishery has been under severe restrictions in order to bring it back. Big game anglers must run far offshore in order to find blue and white marlin, sailfish, yellowfin tuna and other blue-water species.

California

There's a sharp division between milder southern waters and those from San Francisco north. The northern portion of the state is more like Oregon and Washington, primarily concerned with salmon runs rather than standard saltwater fishing. San Francisco Bay is noted for its striped bass fishing, as well as the salmon and sturgeon sport. Southern California has large party boat fleets. Most offshore fishing is around kelp beds and rough bottom for a variety of rockfish and other bottom species plus California halibut, yellowtail, white sea bass,

ABOVE *Throwing a cast net for bait fish from a charter boat off the Florida Keys.*

OPPOSITE ABOVE *A fine red drum (redfish) taken at Empire, Louisiana.*

OPPOSITE BELOW *Anglers boarding the Royal Polaris at San Diego, California.*

bonito, Pacific barracuda and mackerel. During the winter, deep-water bottom fishing is featured. The large party boat fleet at San Diego includes many vessels specially constructed for making runs to distant grounds off Baja California or shorter summer trips for albacore. The latter sometimes come close enough to be caught on day trips, but in other years are only found far offshore. Striped marlin provide the best big game sport in late summer and early fall. Swordfish are also sought after by offshore anglers, as are mako, thresher and blue sharks.

Pacific Northwest

Salmon fishing holds the spotlight from Oregon to Alaska, but this fishing (even that which occurs at sea) is covered in fresh water books and won't be duplicated here. There is also fine jigging and bait fishing offshore for rockfish and other colorful and tasty bottom species, including the highly desired lingcod. Halibut fishing is another feature, especially from Alaskan ports where they are fairly abundant. Striped bass are abundant in the Coos Bay area of Oregon, and some experts suspect that a new all-tackle world record could be caught there.

INDEX

Page numbers in *italics* refer to captions.